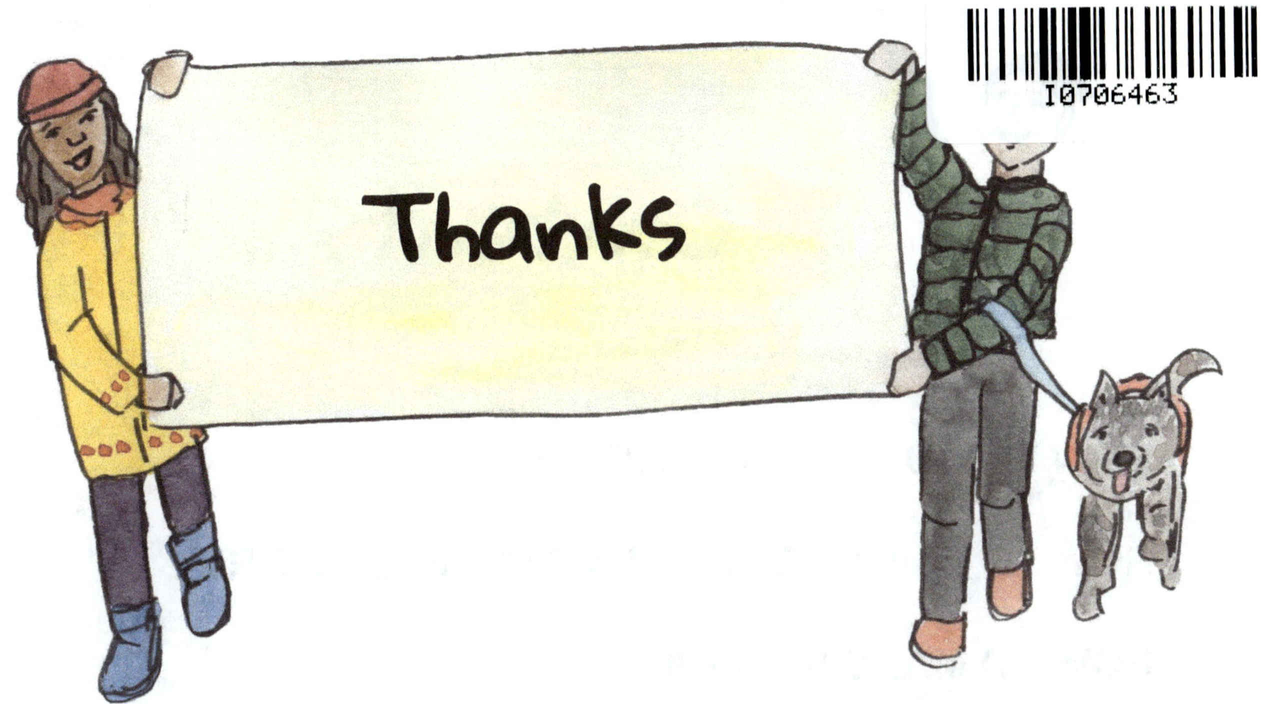

Art always has been for and by the people. Making art isn't just about creating something beautiful, it's about the process of creating community and strengthening our bonds of solidarity.

So we hope you will use this booklet in groups — as a process to refine your strategy and dig deeper into your vision for change.

Much of this booklet was written by material adapted from **David Solnit** — who is an arts organizer, using culture, art, giant puppets and theater in mass mobilizations for popular education and as an organizing tool @davidsolnit — and **Kevin Buckland**, who is part of several horizontal collectives including Artivist Network and Gastivists Collective. **Hannah Gelderman** did all the amazing artwork www.hannahgelderman.com.

Thanks go to **Elizabeth Bates** and **Shemona Moreno** for reviewing. **Daniel Hunter** pulled all the pieces together.

We want this booklet used. Copy. Photocopy. Edit. Do what you want under Creative Commons attribution.

Contents

HOW TO HOST AN ART BUILD

An art build is when a group of people get together to create art for a common project. Art builds are a great way to bring in new volunteers, share work that needs to get done, and get people motivated about an upcoming event! Making art is fun and provides an environment where people can casually get to know each other. Plus, with all this creative energy in the lead up, any event is bound to be more exciting.

This how-to is designed to help you with the logistics of setting up and running an art build. If set up well, it's amazing how much art can be produced quickly with a few volunteers.

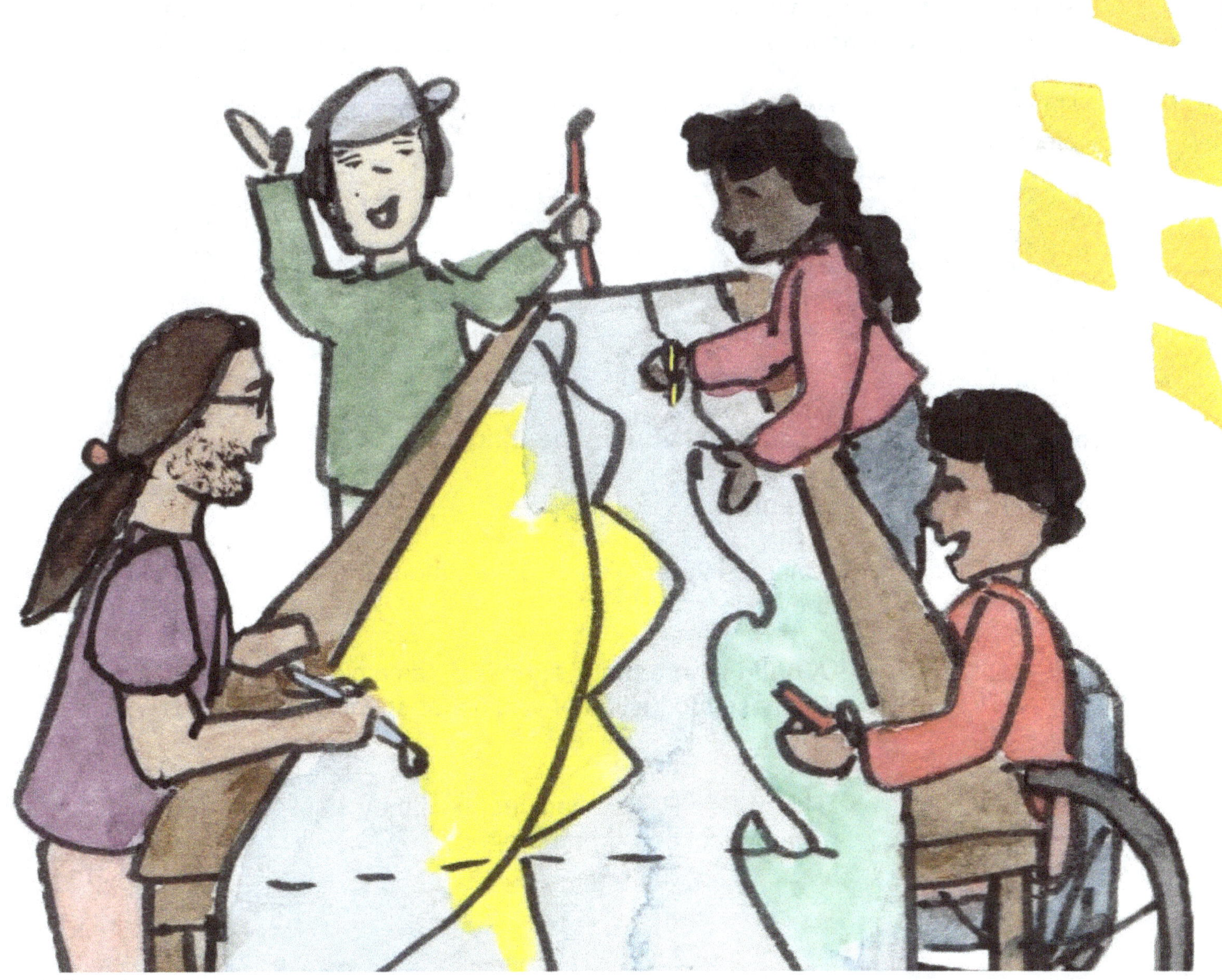

STEP ONE: PREPARE

Find a location

- Art builds can be held just about anywhere, but your needs depend on what you are planning to make. Places that it's okay get a little paint on the floor (such as garages, warehouses, basements, etc.) can make the build less stressful.

- If the art build is part of a conference or in a rented space perhaps they have an outdoor space, a loading dock, or basement you can use (rented places often charge for stray paint).

- Generally you want a location where you have easy access to running water, toilets and electrical outlets.

- Outdoor and public spaces are often great as they attract a crowd (just be conscious of electrical needs you might have, and access to water and toilets).

- Having a flat floor to work on is useful for painting on fabric (especially big pieces).

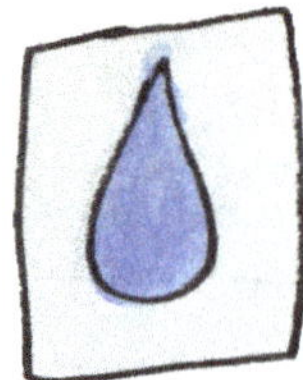 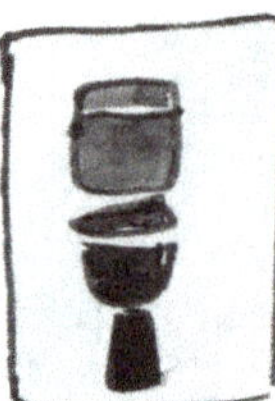 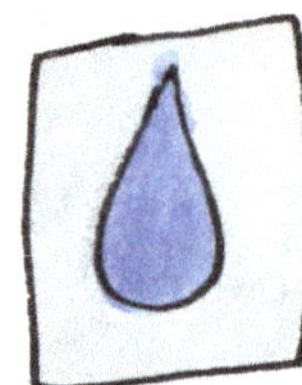 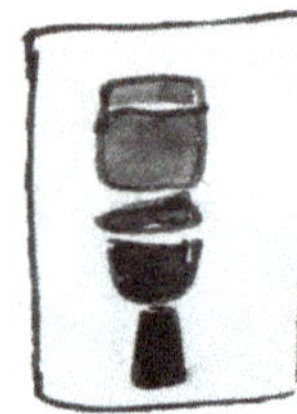 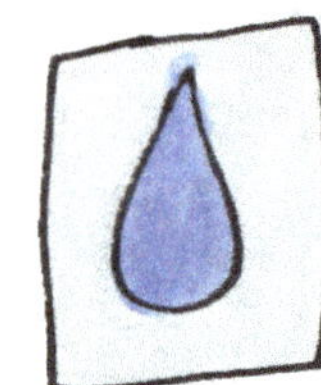 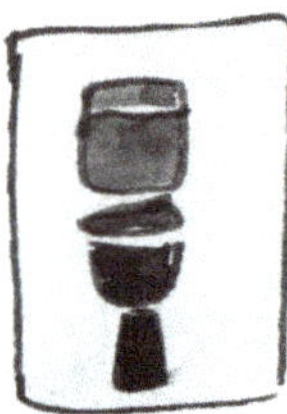

Determine what type of art build you are hosting

There are 3 types of art builds:

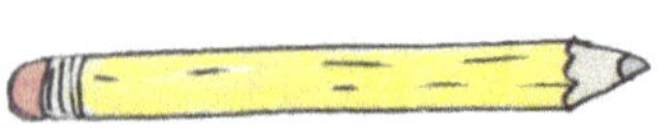

Laissez- Faire: You provide materials and people do what they like.

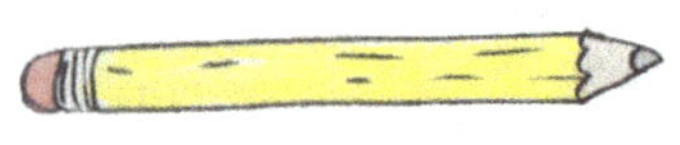

A build with a plan: The build has a clear goal. Often used for mass production of visuals, or specific things for an event.

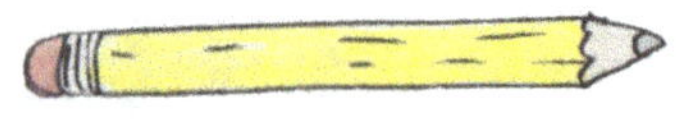

The mixer: People can choose if they want to work on their own project or a group project.

Volunteers and schedule

- If you are hosting a build with a plan make sure you have a clear plan ahead of time, and know what your priorities are (e.g., X should be made before Y!). Know how many of each thing you would like to make and have enough supplies.

- You can make a schedule and let people know when you need volunteers (e.g., setup, cleanup), and then ask volunteers to sign up for specific time slots. You can also get people to volunteer beforehand to make snacks or collect supplies.

- If you are hosting a laissez-faire or mixer, you can also host it as a 'drop in anytime' art build so people can come whenever works for them.

Samples and instructions

- If you are running "a build with a plan" it is a good idea to make samples of what you want people to make, so have these ready beforehand.

- Depending on what you are making you might want instructions printed or written out for people to follow. It will help to let people know who to ask if they have questions or need support.

- If you are doing a banner or something with a specific design, have the design ready and banner 'maps' for people to follow along as they paint.

- If possible, make all stencils and woodcuts/cardboard cuts ahead of time (and have a copy available in case something happens to the original).

Invite local press

- If your planned action is legal and being publicized, invite local press to your art build. Art builds are generally very photogenic events, and can be a great way to get press before your event, which can be a great outreach tool to boost attendance at your event.

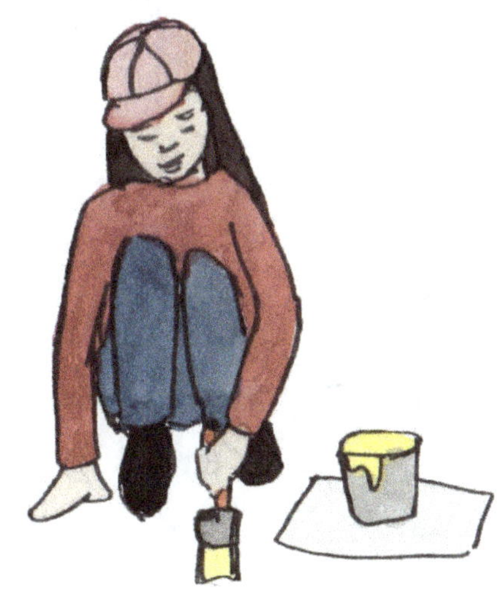

Materials and supplies

The materials you will need depend on what you are doing, but here is an overview of materials that are useful for an art build. Make sure you have all your supplies ready before the art build, and write your own list with any additional supplies that you need.

For a few more tips on how to get free materials see the 'basic materials for extraordinary beauty' notes following this list!

Set-up
- Tables
- Plastic for floor
- Drop cloths
- Broom/mop

Painting
- Paint
- Brushes (many)
- Small containers such as yogurt containers
    - lids are nice to store unused paint
    - you can also cut the top off soda bottles
- Rollers and trays
- Smocks
- Water bucket(s)
- Rags

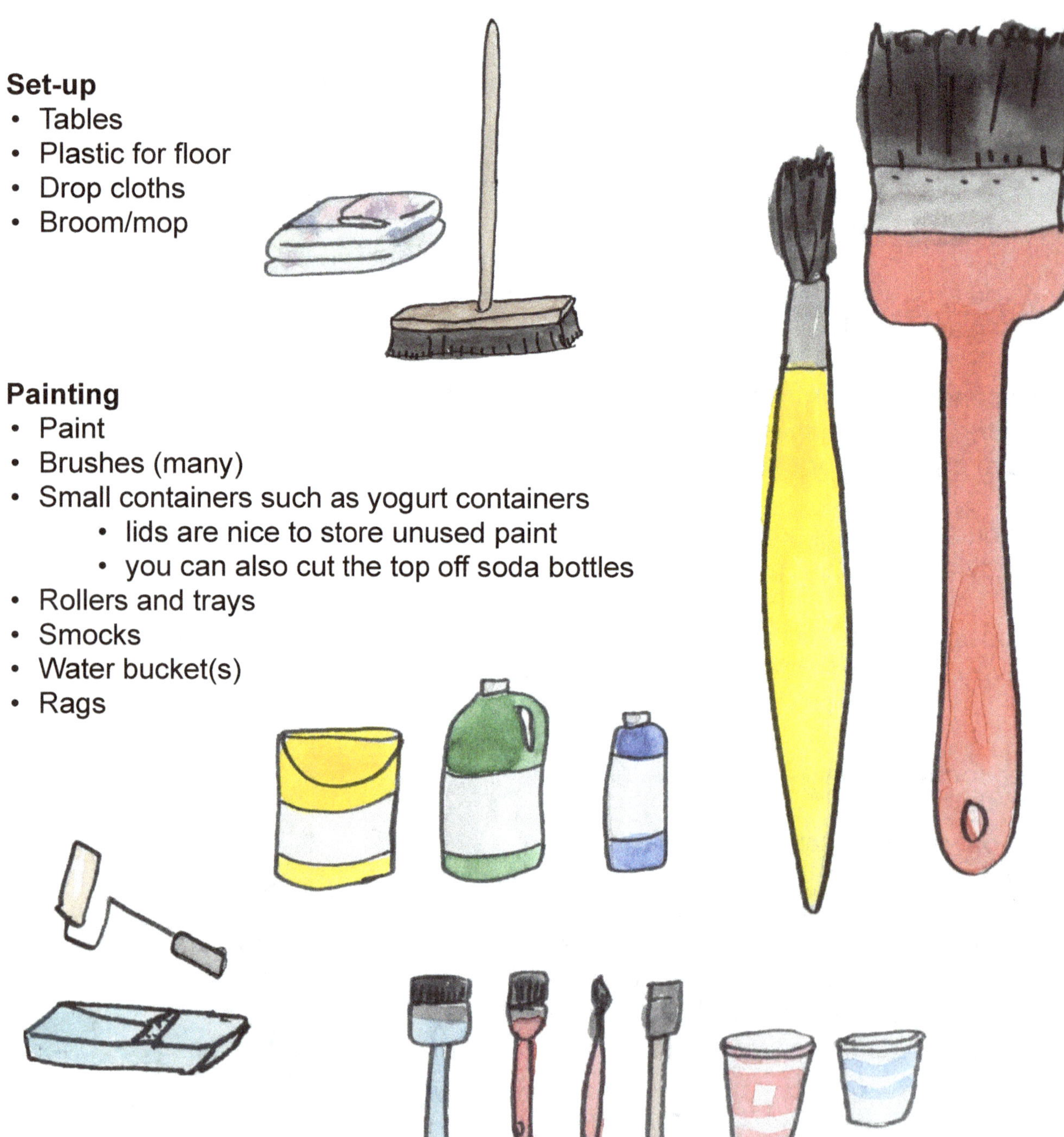

Drying line

- Clothesline or string
- Clothes pins, safety pins or clips
- Plastic or drop cloth

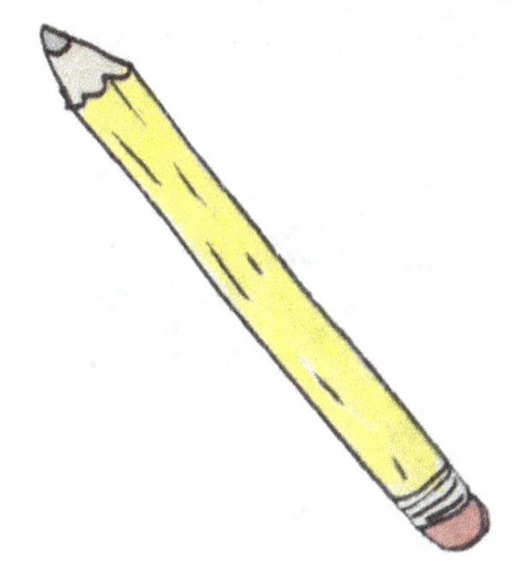

Tools

- Scissors
- Utility knife/x-acto and extra blades
- Drill and bits
- Saw
- Pencils and erasers
- Scrap paper for sketching
- Permanent markers
- Chalk
- Sewing machine
- Thread and extra needles
- Measuring tape and ruler or straight edge

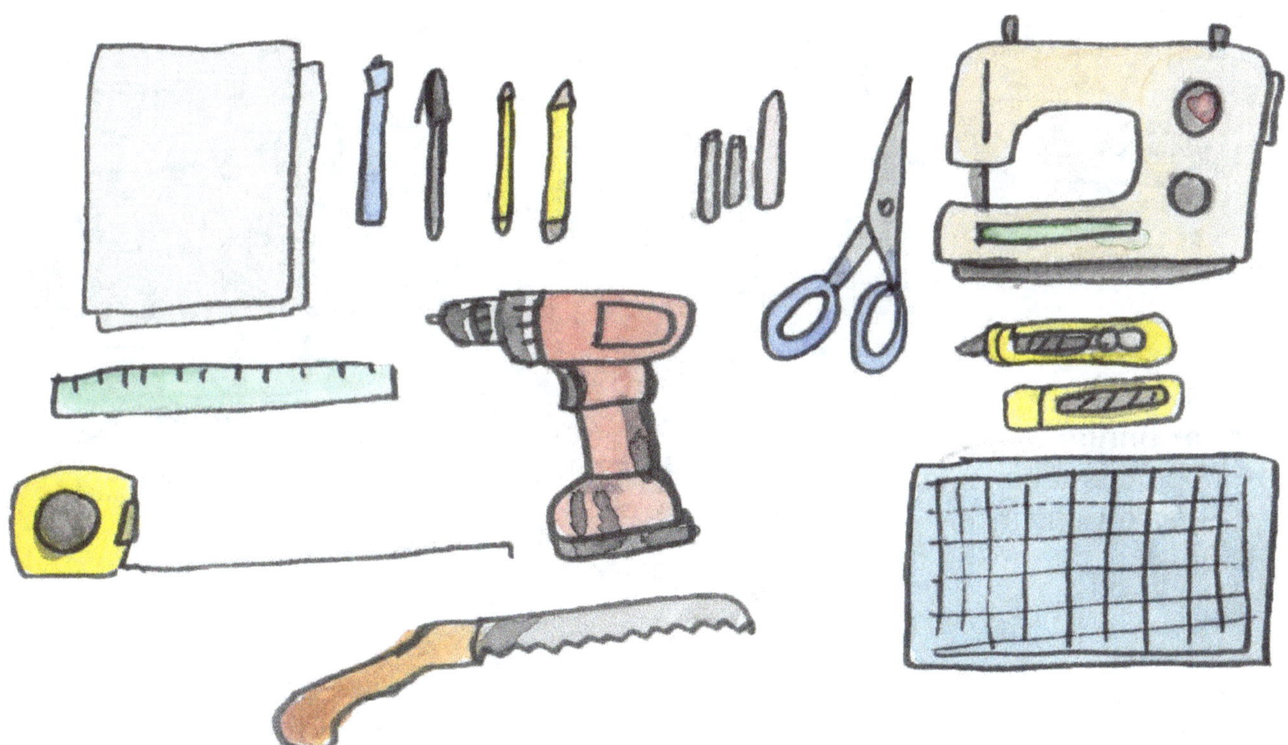

Fasteners

- Staple gun/stapler
- Staple pliers
- Staples
- String/twine
- Hardware (nuts, bolts, etc.)
- Tape -- duct tape, masking tape
- Wire (wire clothes hangers)
- Glue/wheat paste
- Hot glue gun and glue
- Rubber ties (from bicycle inner tubes)

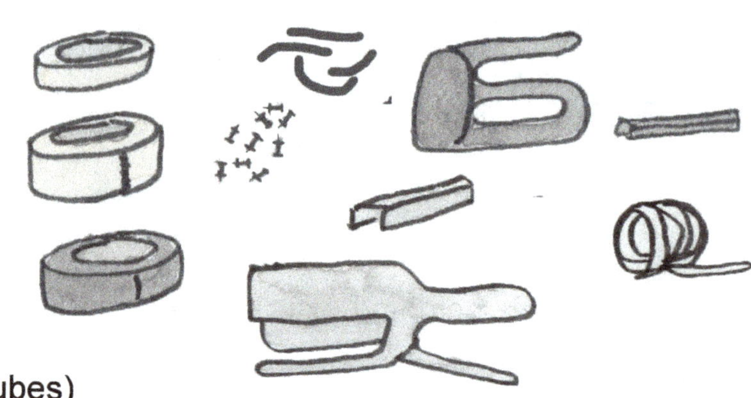

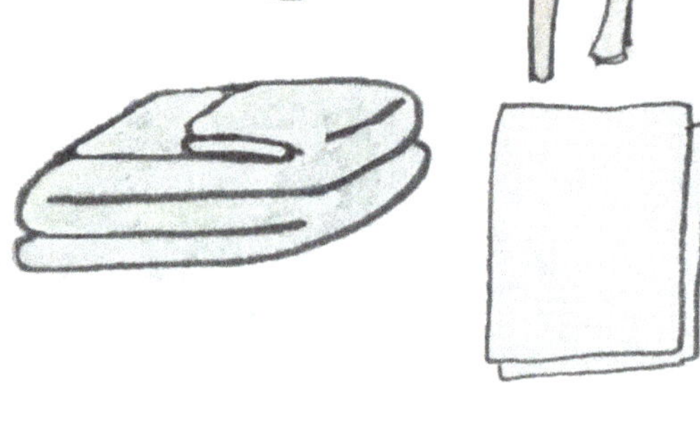

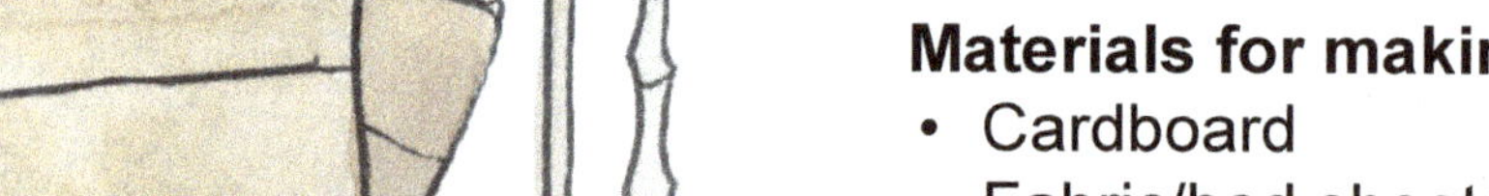

Materials for making

- Cardboard
- Fabric/bed sheets
- Sticks and poles
- Paper/poster board
- Plastic for stencils

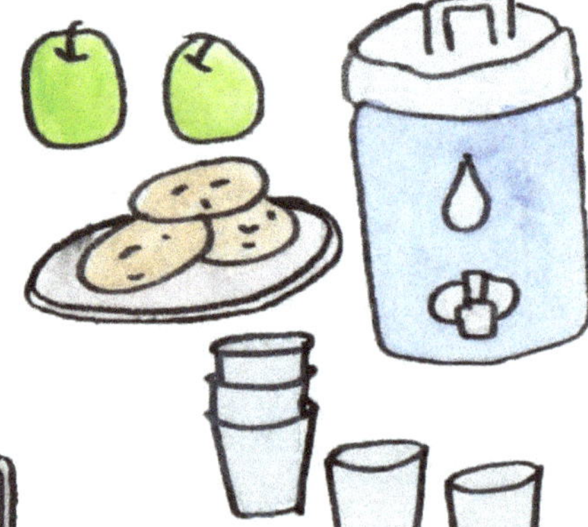

Other things

- Laptop and projector
- Speaker and music
- Snacks

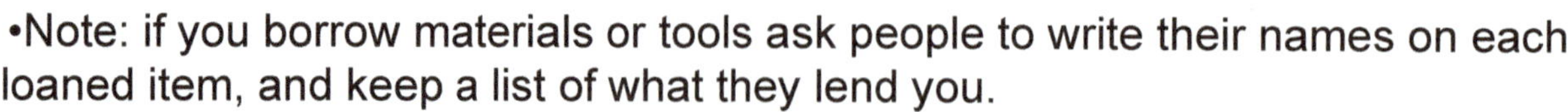

•Note: if you borrow materials or tools ask people to write their names on each loaned item, and keep a list of what they lend you.

Basic Materials for Extraordinary Beauty

Literally anything can be used to create art. The materials listed here are some of the most versatile and easy to come by. So much can be made almost entirely out of garbage - a manifestation of the belief that creativity can turn even a pile of garbage (or an unsustainable society) into something beautiful and productive.

Cardboard

You can make just about anything out of cardboard. Large pieces can often be found in the dumpsters behind stores that sell large things (refrigerators, big chairs, or car windshields) or ask inside the store.

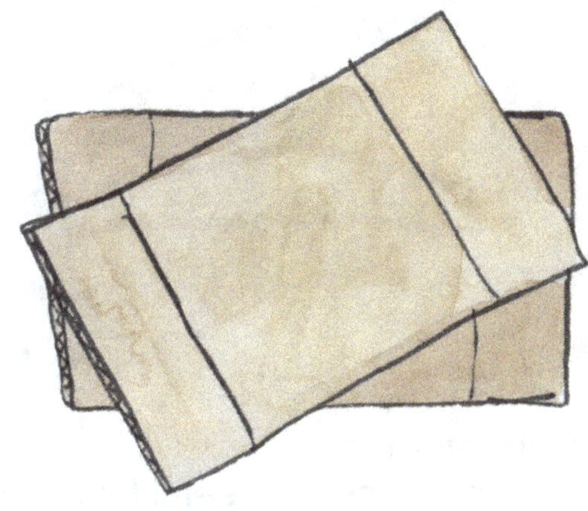

Paint

Almost everything can be painted using regular latex water-based house paint. Ask around, it is very common for people to have left-over paint they are happy to give away. Or ask paint stores if they have mis-mixed paint. Fabric can be dyed using a mixture of lots of water and latex paint. If you buy paint get primary colors (red, yellow, blue) from which you can mix other colors. Strong colors are best -- you can always add white.

Fabric

Used bed sheets are great and are frequently thrown out by hotels. Call or stop by a few hotels to ask if you can have their stained or ripped sheets.

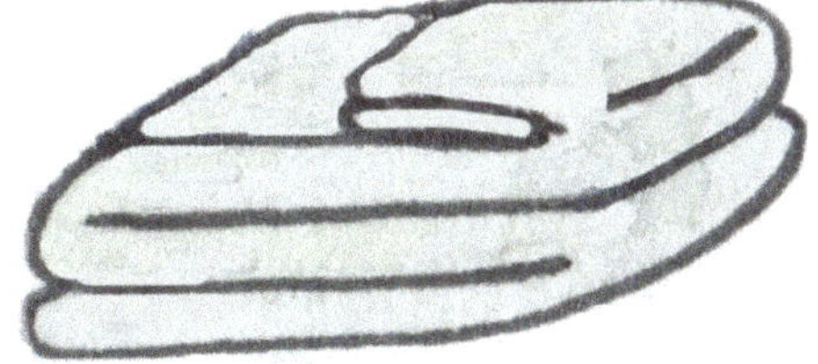

Rubber ties
A great material for attaching things together is strips of
rubber (because elastic doesn't slip). You can make
rubber ties by cutting up bicycle inner tubes into strips of
rubber. Go to any bike shop at the end of the day and
they probably have burst inner tubes to throw out.

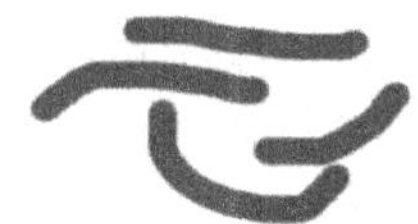

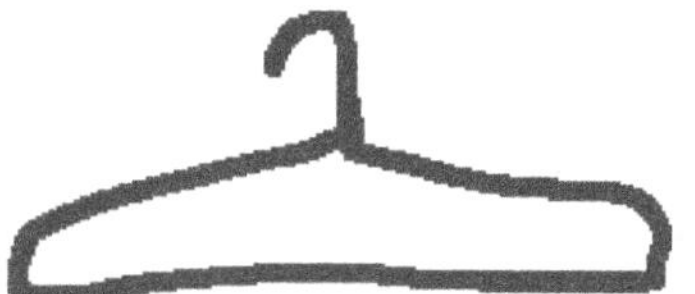

Wire
Wire can be useful for hanging and
attaching. Just cut the top off wire clothes
hangers for some good strong wire.

Wooden poles
Wooden poles are useful for anything you want to get up high or anything big you
want to make. Bamboo is great because it is lightweight, but any straight tree
branch or broomstick works too.

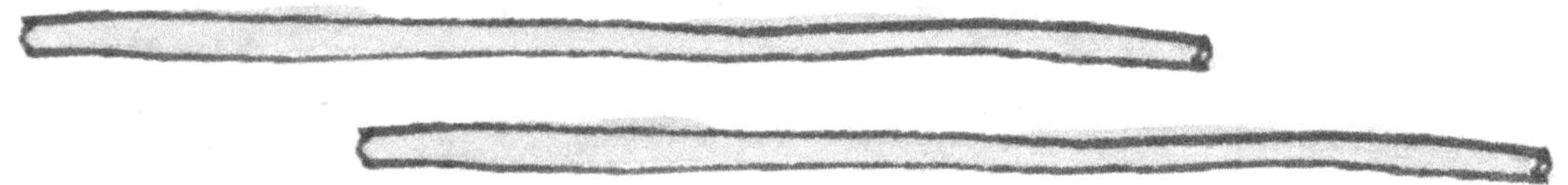

STEP TWO: SET UP YOUR ART BUILD

Putting a little time and thought into preparing the space will make an art build run much more efficiently.

Tables

If you can, get or make some tables as it is often more comfortable to work on a table than on the floor. Tables can be made easily by putting pieces of plywood, wood, or an old door on top of saw horses, chairs, garbage cans, or sturdy cardboard boxes.

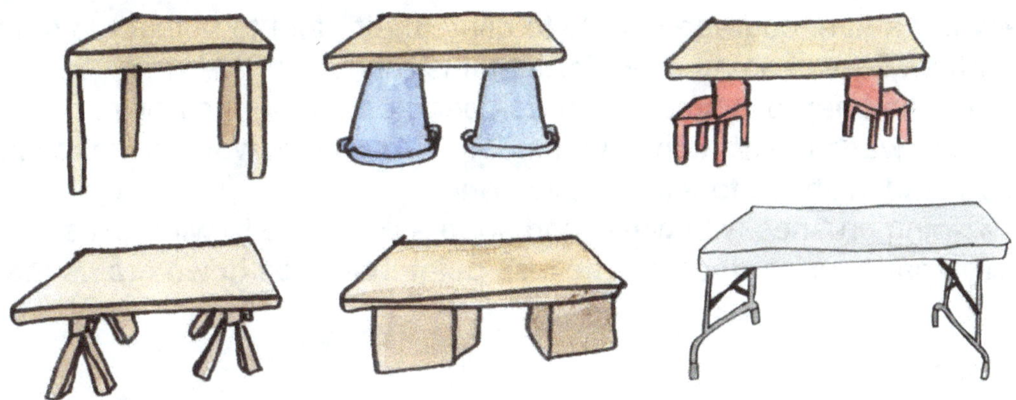

Protecting what needs to be protected

Things can get messy when you have many people using paint in the same space. Cover or remove anything that needs to stay pristine. You can use a roll of thick plastic and tape it down onto the floor. This is a good investment as it makes drips and spills much easier to clean up and can be reused. You can put down cardboard, too, or drop cloths.

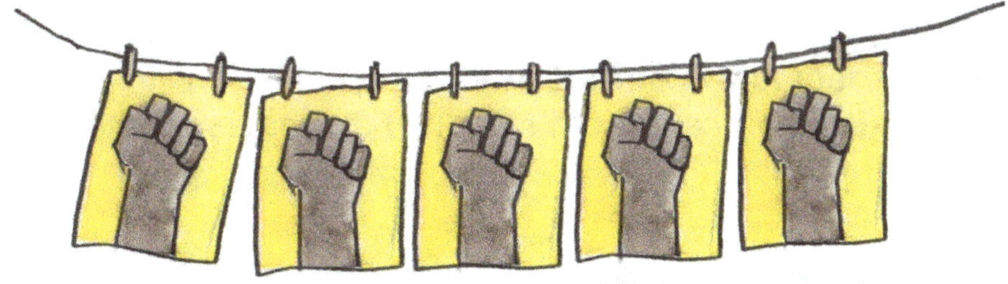

Drying lines

If you are going to be painting on fabric or paper, setting up some drying lines will give you a space to hang things to dry. Put plastic, cardboard or drop cloth underneath in case things drip, or set up the drying line outside.

Stations

- Setting up clearly designated stations (i.e., areas for specific uses) will help to keep things organized, and will facilitate people working in teams. It will also give tools and materials a "home" so people know where to find things.
- You and a few organizers or volunteers should arrive early and set up the space before your official start time so that when people arrive ready to paint, you are ready for them!

Paint station
- Keep all your paint in one place. Provide small containers so people can bring some of whatever color they need with them, but ask people to leave large paint containers at the paint station.
- Provide water and encourage people to dilute their paint to help it run smoothly and go further, but not so much water that it is runny!
- Provide rags and perhaps smocks, or ask people to bring their own.
- Ask people to wash their brushes when done. You might want to make signs for all this so you don't have to tell it to everyone.
- Before washing brushes with water and soap ask people to wipe excess paint off on scrap paper or cardboard. The less paint that goes down drains the better.

Tool station
- This can be a place for many useful items such as tape, string, drills, scissors, utility knives, tools, etc.

Garbage/ recycling station:
- Set up an area with clearly marked garbage cans and recycling cans

Any other station specific to your art build
- Maybe a sewing station, a cardboard station… or whatever other sort of station you need!

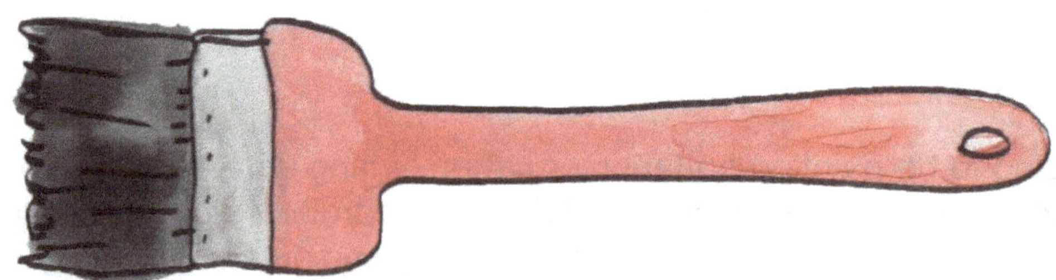

Working area

- Have spaces ready for people to work at, and maybe divide up the 'work' areas into stations too, e.g., a stencil station, a paint station, etc. Do whatever makes sense for your art build.
- It can be helpful to divide the working area into a painting (wet materials) area and a building (dry materials) area so there isn't paint everywhere.

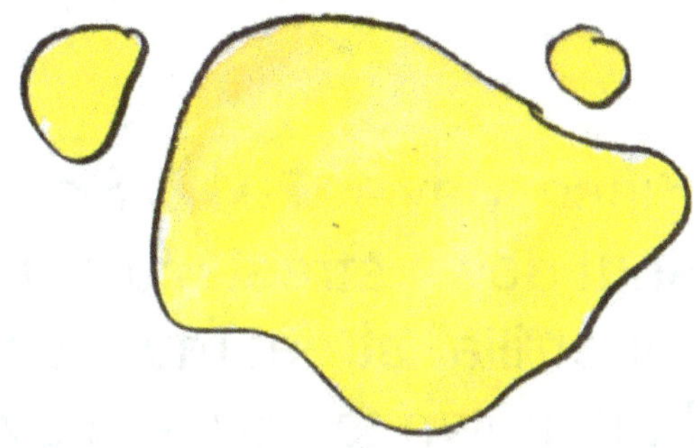

Running an art build

- Create an energizing atmosphere and make sure people are comfortable. Play some music and let people know where they can find snacks and hang out for a break.

- Feel free to make loud announcements instead of saying something 50 times. Ask for help if you need it.

- You also want to be on the lookout for two things: paint brushes that are drying out and paint spills (someone stepping in spilled paint, then walking around, can be a nightmare to clean) and get those cleaned up quickly!

- Take lots of pictures and have fun!

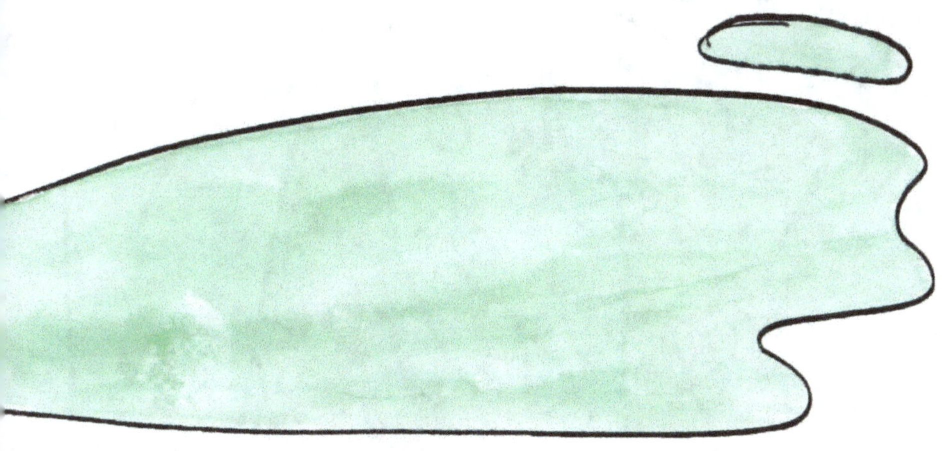

HOW TO PAINT A TEMPORARY STREET MURAL

Since May 1, 2012, San Francisco Bay Area movements have shut down streets to car traffic and created unpermitted or "guerrilla" street murals to lift up critical struggles. This tactic has grown to be used by many movements. In 2020 the Black Lives Matter movement made giant street murals, often with permanent paint, which sparked the City of DC painting giant yellow letters spelling "Black Lives Matter" in front of the Trump White House.

In this way, street murals can reclaim space in a hopeful and beautiful way. They are a powerful tactic that can inspire and mobilize people, while also sharing stories of the community. Planning, training, preparing, and painting together are great ways to build skills, strengthen groups and foster community.

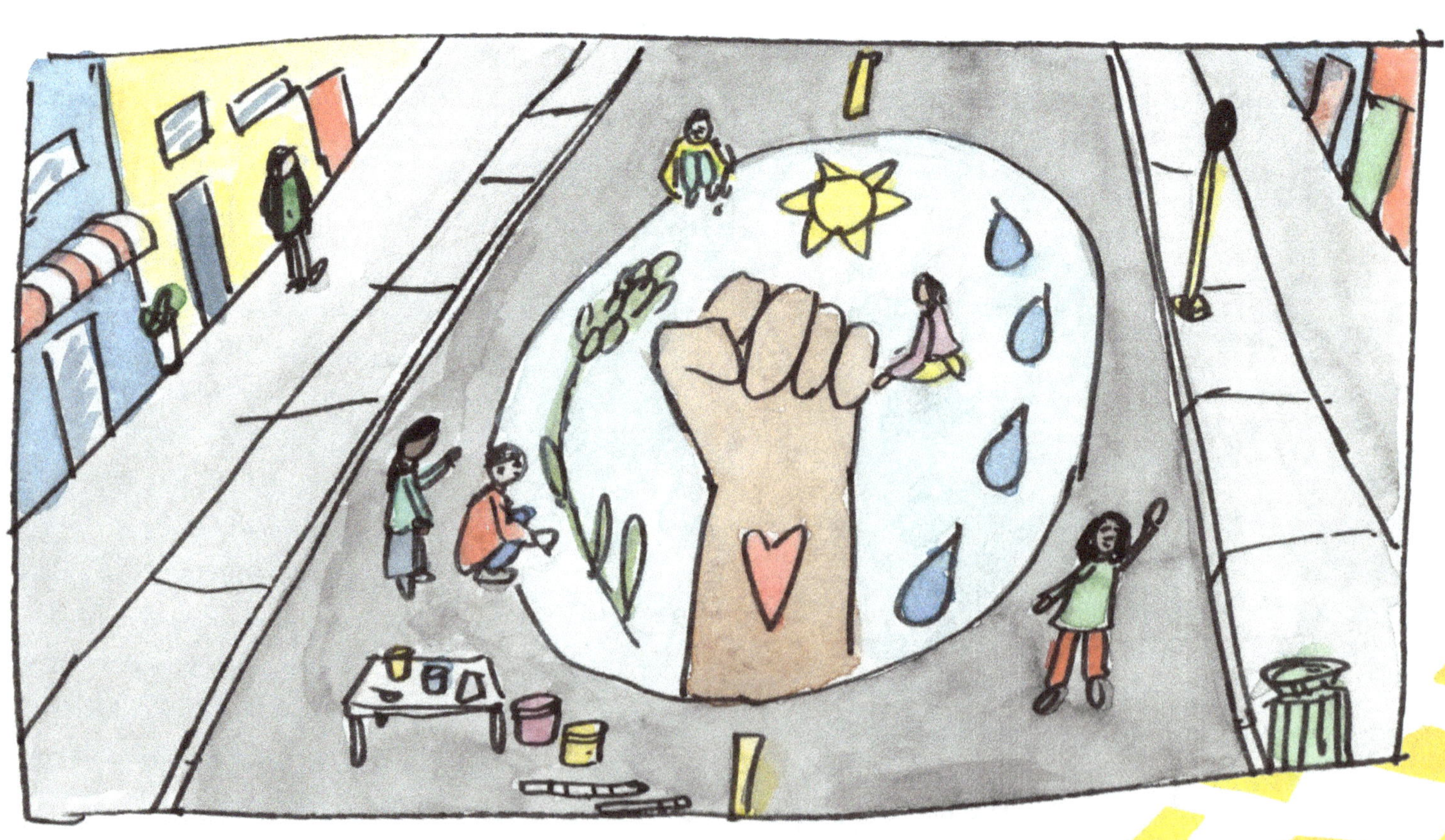

SUPPLIES

- **Non toxic tempera or clay paint**
  - For a temporary mural the paint needs to be able to wash away, so it should be washable and non-toxic. Both clay paint and tempera paint work well for temporary street murals. (Do not use house paint.)

  - **Clay paint**
    You can make clay paint yourself by drying out ceramic clay or clay soil. You can buy clay from art or pottery retailers, or if you have clay soils or deposits locally, you can collect clay yourself. Some groups have also collected charcoal from fires to create black paint. Soak the clay overnight in water in a 5 gallon/20 liter plastic bucket and then mix using a paint mixing attachment on a corded drill. Add water to get the desired consistency--thin so it will paint easily and dry faster, but not so watery that the color is weak. You can usually get clays in natural or earthy colours such as grays, whites, reds and browns.

  - **Tempera paint**
    Tempera paint is the kind of water soluble paint kids use in school (because it's non-toxic). It comes in a wide range of colors and also a range of quality--some brands or types cover better and have stronger colors than others. Art supply stores and some stores that carry toys or craft supplies may carry tempera paint. You can buy tempera paint in a powder and mix it yourself or you can buy it in liquid form ready to go.

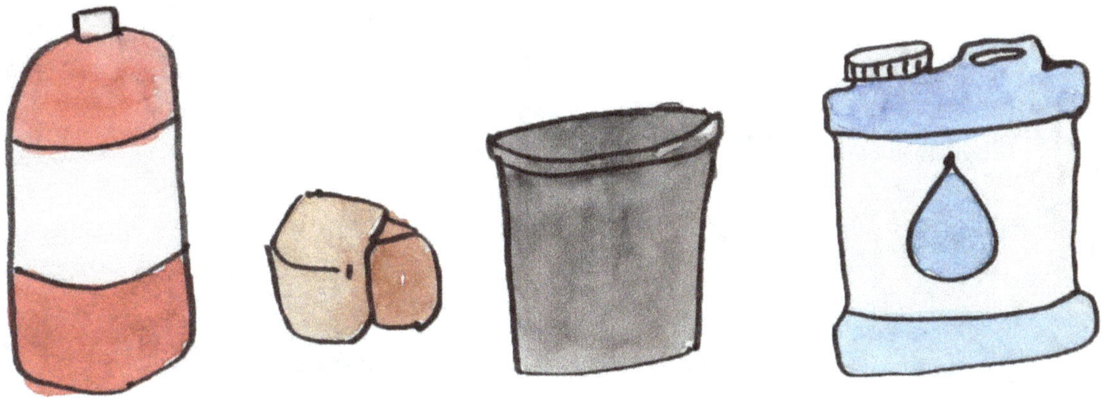

- **Buckets**
    - 3 or 5 gallon/10- 20 liter buckets with lids for pre-mixing paint in advance with water.
    - one or more 3 or 5 gallon /10- 20 liter bucket(s) for cleaning brushes.

- **Small reusable containers**
  Use these to divide up paint between people, e.g., yogurt containers or wide cups. Make sure the opening is wide enough for your brushes to fit. Lids may be useful, too.

- **Paint brushes**
  Have a variety of sizes and lots of big brushes. Think about how many people will be painting at once and buy enough brushes for everyone.

- **Broom** (for cleaning the area before painting)
- **Cardboard & camping/gardening mats** (for people's knees as you paint)
- **Water** (for thinning paint and washing brushes)
- **Rags** (for wiping up spills and drips and wiping hands)

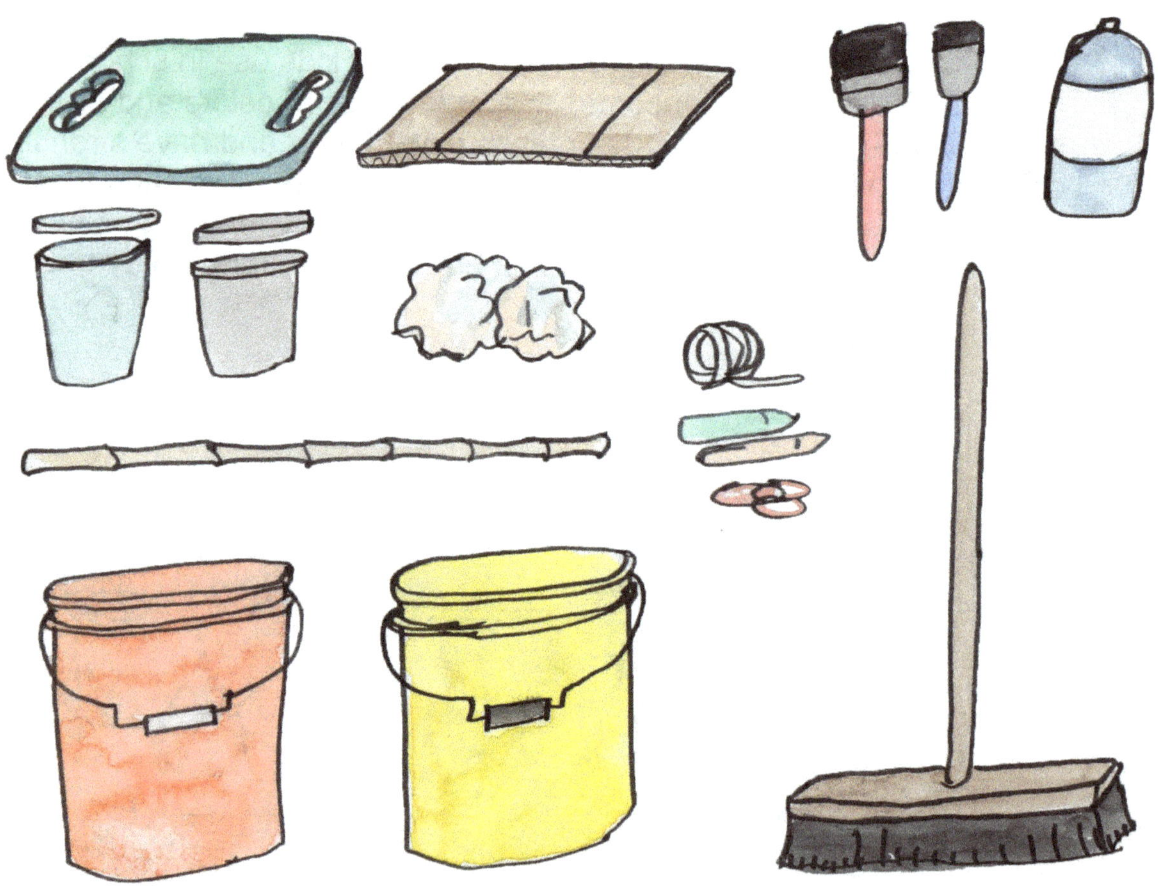

- **Long bamboo stick** (4-5 ft/1.5 m to make DIY chalk holders, so you can stand while chalking)
- **Sidewalk chalk** (for chalking out your design)
- **Heavy string** (100 ft /30 m to use while chalking your circles)
- **Elastic bands** (to tie around sticks and chalk to secure the chalk)

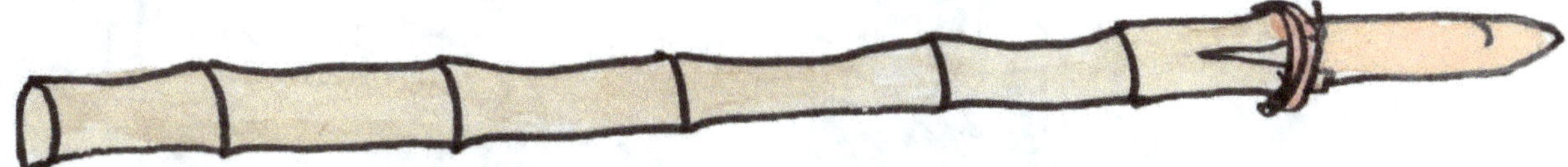

- **Clipboards or cardboard and tape (**to attach designs to while you are working)
- **Printouts** of the mural 'map'
- **Hospitality items (**snacks and water, extra sunscreen - or whatever is weather-appropriate - for volunteers.)
- **Portable speakers and music** (if you don't have song leaders)
- **Megaphone** (if you will be talking to a large group or crowd)
- **Safety items** (vests for marshals or liaisons, pylons if you need them)
- **A way to identify organizers** (t-shirts, arm bands, etc.)
- **Fold up tables and wagons/carts** to easily move and place your supplies.
- **Ladder** - for taking a photo!

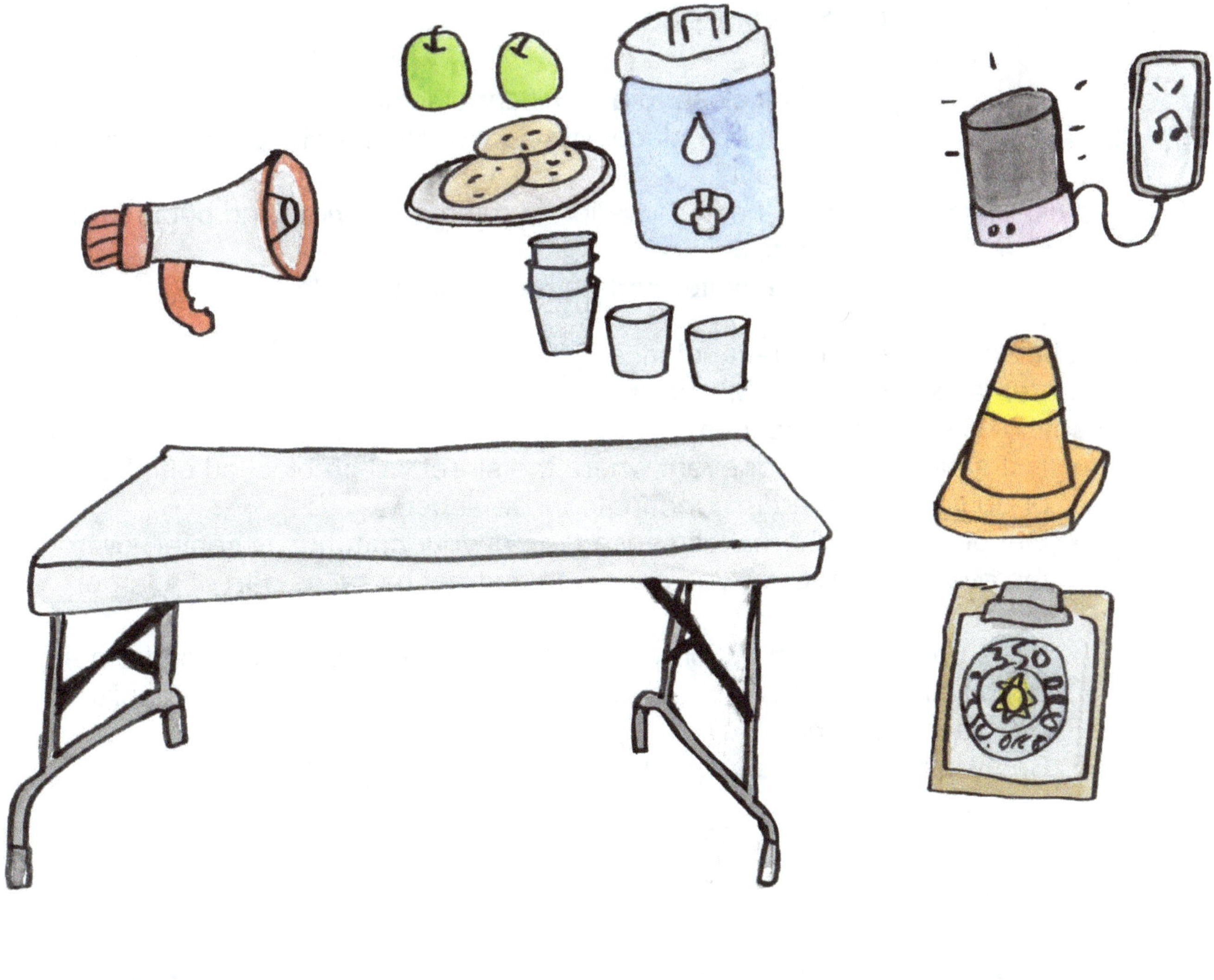

STEP ONE: CHOOSE A LOCATION

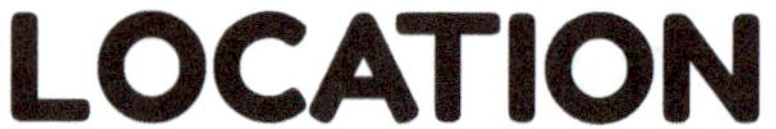

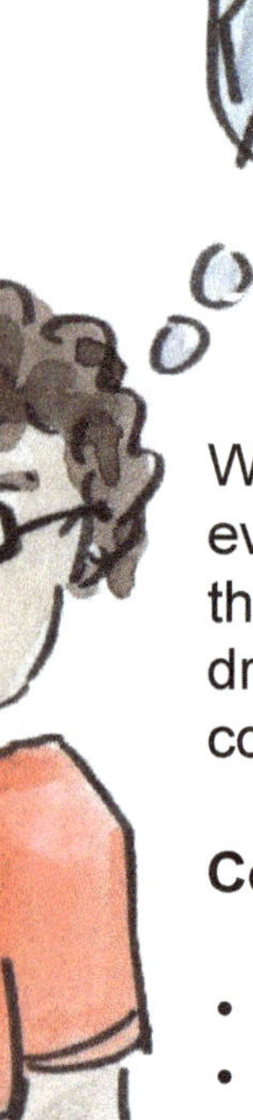

Where will you paint the street mural? The purpose of the event or mural painting can definitely help you determine this. Some possibilities include public squares, sidewalks, driveways, parking lots, schools, community centers, or, of course, streets.

Consider:

- Is it close to a significant location?
- Is it in a place with a lot of community people who will see it?
- Is there a location to get a good view and photo from above?
- Are water and bathrooms nearby ?

- Will it be seen by your target audience?
- Is the area accessible by public transit?
- Is it safe? Safety considerations:
    - Is it a part of a rally or event where the street will be blocked off already or do you also need to coordinate these aspects?
    - Get permission if it makes sense (i.e., at your community center) or from the event organizers if you are doing a street mural as part of a larger event.
    - If it is part of a direct action you might not be asking permission from the city or officials, but you should coordinate closely with event organizers and safety liaisons.
    - Be aware of any local regulations regarding street art.

STEP TWO: DESIGN YOUR MURAL

- You can design the mural collaboratively with your group or community, or hire an artist from the community to create a design for you.

- Choose the message and story you want to share and think of what words and images will communicate that message.

- Remember:
  - High contrast (such as light text on dark background) makes images and words pop and be more visible.
  - It's great to include both images and words to tell your story!
  - Keep it simple – make it quick and easy to read, this also makes it easier to paint – especially if it is your first mural. Also, plan your design (and mural size) according to how much time you will have to paint the mural.
  - Circle designs are great because there are some easy ways to lay out circle designs on the street.

- Do a practice run! Even if you do a mini version on a driveway or sidewalk, it's amazingly helpful actually to practice laying it out, getting paint ready, working with your team, and painting.

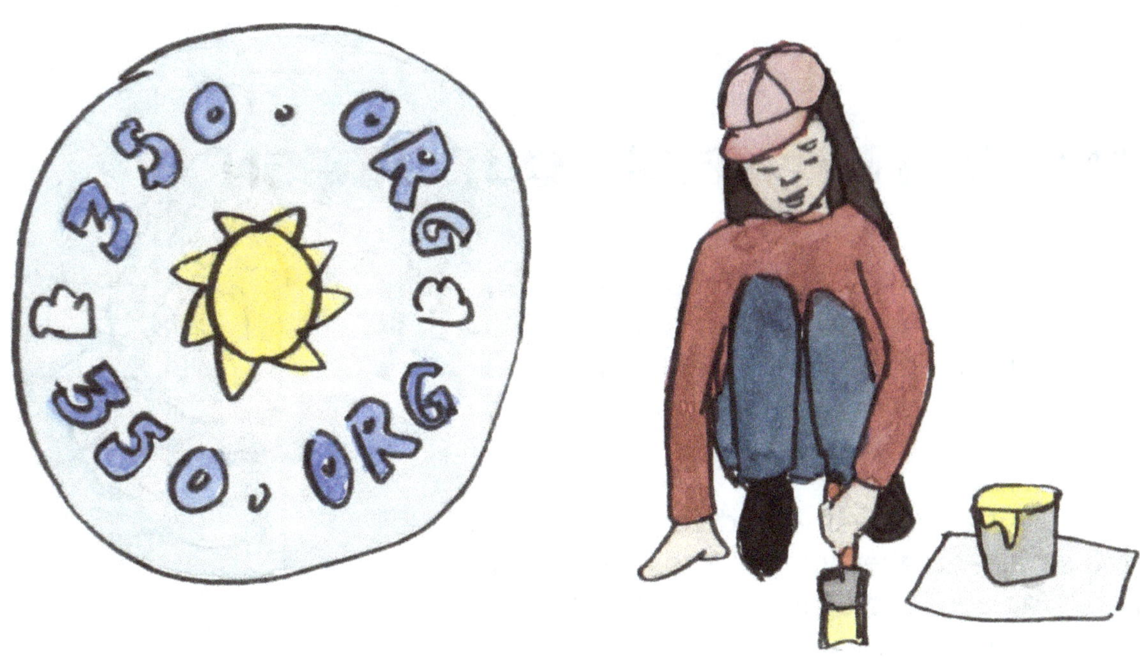

Preparing paint:

- Estimate how much paint and how much of each color you need:
    - For a 35-foot/10-meter across circular mural you can estimate you will need about 3- 4 gallons/11- 15 liters of paint to cover the entire area.
    - To help figure out the amount you will need of each paint color estimate what percentage of the mural each color is.
    - Pre-mix your paint before the event. You want everything to be as ready as possible before you start. Store and carry your mixed paint in containers or buckets with lids.

- Mix to the right consistency. It should flow smoothly across concrete but not be too drippy!

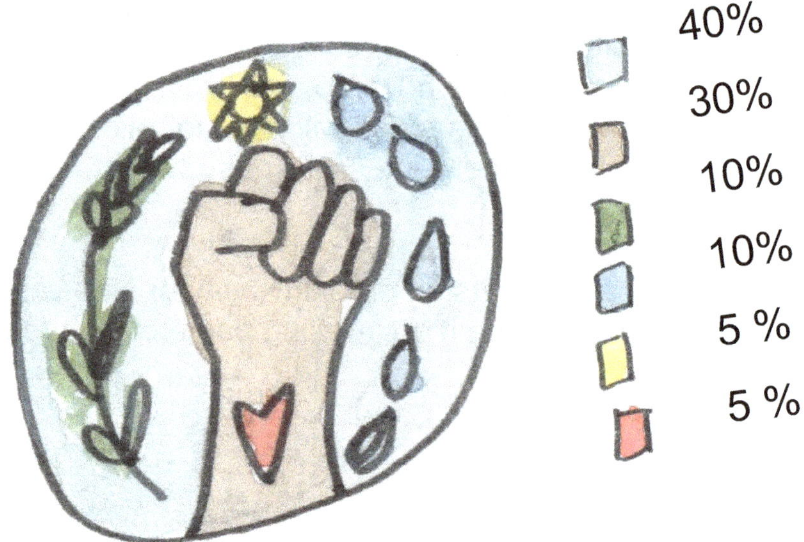

WAYS TO TRANSFER YOUR DESIGN

There are a few different processes you can use to transfer your design onto the street. Bring the supplies for whichever method you choose!

Grid method:
You can draw a grid over your design (don't make the grid too small -- it takes longer) and use chalk to grid your painting space to scale. Then you have a reference for copying each section of the design to the painting space.

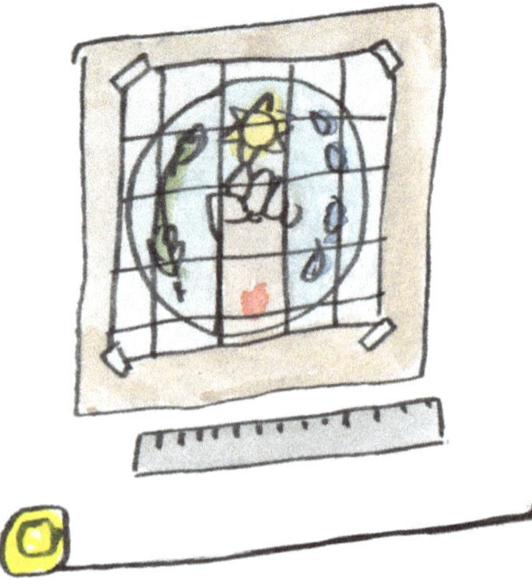

Templates:
If you have complicated images, you could choose to cut the shape(s) out of paper
the size you want for your mural and then trace them onto the ground with chalk.
You can get large paper rolls from art stores or flooring paper from hardware
stores. Beforehand, you could project your image onto the paper to trace and then
cut out the shape.

Circle Grid:
If you have designed your mural as a circle you can use a human-string-chalk
compass to chalk out your circles.

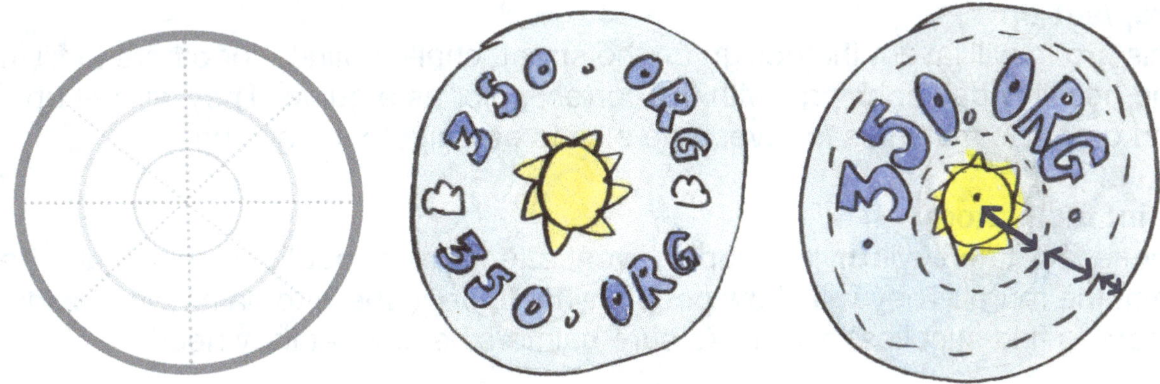

- Have one person hold one end of the string securely in the center of the circle.
  They can loop this end around a bamboo pole that they are holding, or their leg,
  so that it will move in a circle. Measure out the string to the radius of your mural.
  Have a second person tie the end of the measured string to the bamboo/chalk
  pole. The second person can pull the string taut and chalk the circumference of
  the circle on the ground while the first person continues to secure the string at
  the center.

- You can chalk out additional circles inside, as needed for your design. You could
  mark out the tops and bottoms of words or images that go around in a circle. If
  transferring an image from your sketch, you can, for example, measure and
  make circles on your sketch for every 5 ft/1.5 m in from the outer circumference
  (for example, one each at 5 ft/1.5 m in from the outer edge, 10 ft/3m in and 15
  ft/4.5m). You can also divide the circle across in quarters or eighths like a pie to
  help divide up the design within the space.

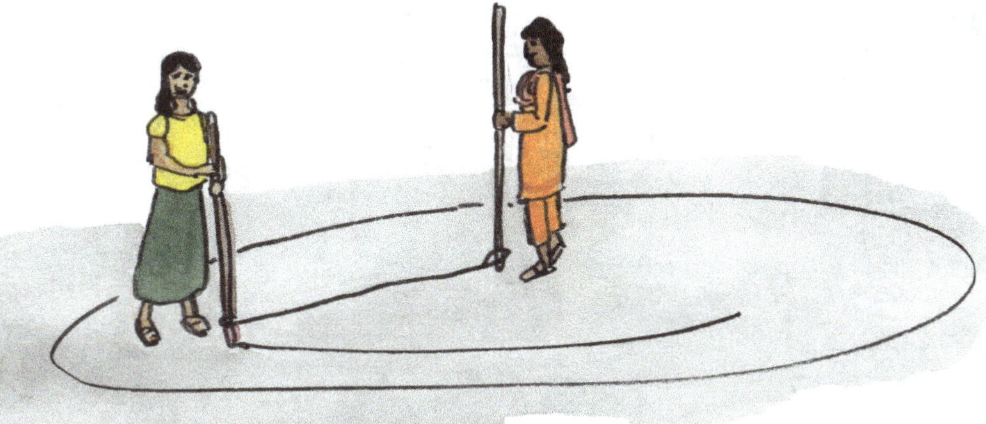

STEP THREE: PREPARE

Supplies:
- Prepare and gather all your supplies in advance of the mural painting day.
- Make sure your design, mural maps, and transfer plan are ready to go!

Roles:
Make sure you have a few people (or more) for each role. Street murals are a great way to get lots of volunteers involved!

- **Prep/set-up**
  This group will layout the design on the street, chalk outlines for others to fill in, and possibly dab each part with the correct color as a guide. They will set up and organize materials for everyone else to participate in painting.

- **Paint facilitators**
  These facilitators will invite people (event attendees or public) to join in and help paint the mural. They will show people what to do, (where to paint, what colors, where to find supplies) and make sure painters have what they need.

- **Police/public liaison**
  These folks will communicate with police or others about what you are doing, and make sure to keep it peaceful and keep the mural space safe.

- **Street safety**
  This team will make sure the mural area is safely blocked off from vehicles so the muralists can safely focus and paint.

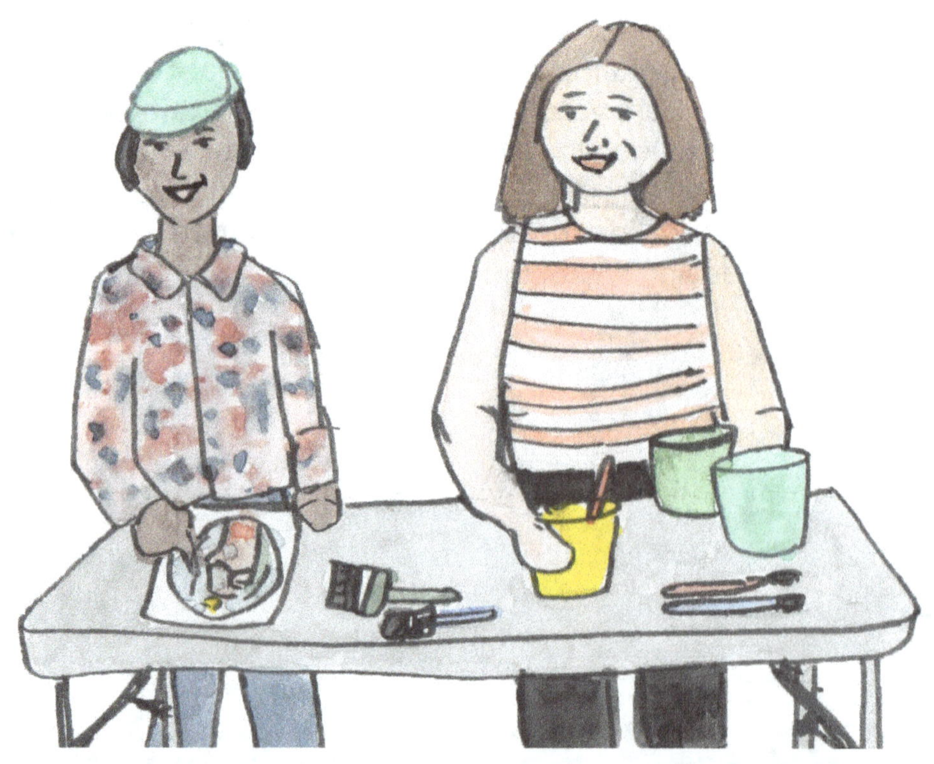

Optional, but encouraged roles…

- **Storytellers**
  These folks will tell the story of the mural -- and the community, movement, or group -- to the public. These can also be your mural team's media spokespeople.

- **Song leaders**
  Does your group or community have song leaders who can lead song while the mural is happening?

- **Documenters (photographers and social media folks)**
  People to take photos and capture the event, both to share immediately on social media, and to amplify your story with a visual record afterwards.

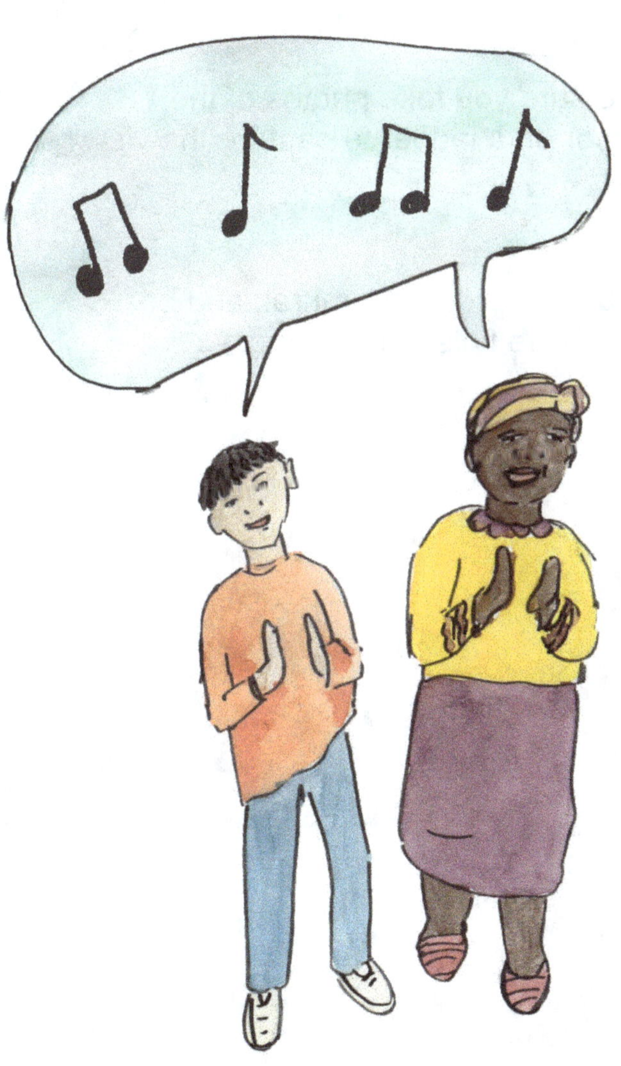

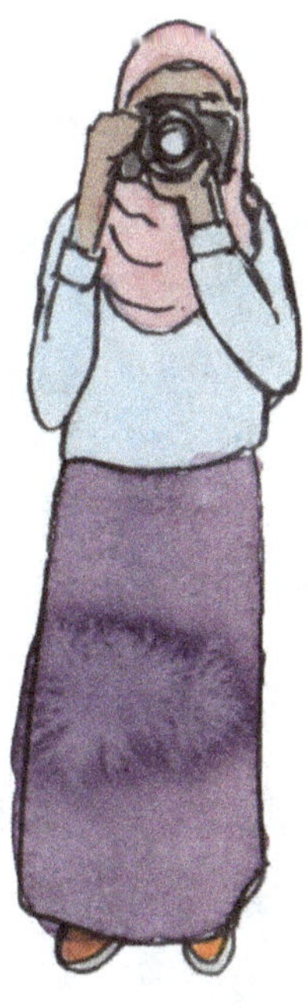

STEP FOUR: CREATE THE MURAL!

On the day of the mural painting bring all your supplies to the site early and make sure all your volunteers are ready!

- **Layout your mural**
  Have your prep volunteers lay out the mural design with chalk and organize all the materials before any painting starts. Others can join these folks to actually paint the mural after the chalk outline has been drawn. Have people draw from the center outwards, to minimize walking on the mural.

- **Facilitate your mural painting**
  It's up to your team to facilitate the painting of your mural--invite other folks to help you and offer them clear directions to give to participants.

- **Celebrate and take photos**
  Take photos throughout, but definitely make sure you take photos of the completed mural. Try to get up in a building or on a ladder to capture the view from above.

- **Clean up all supplies**
  Keep track of your supplies, wipe up any spills outside your mural, and be responsible for removing supplies when you have finished painting.

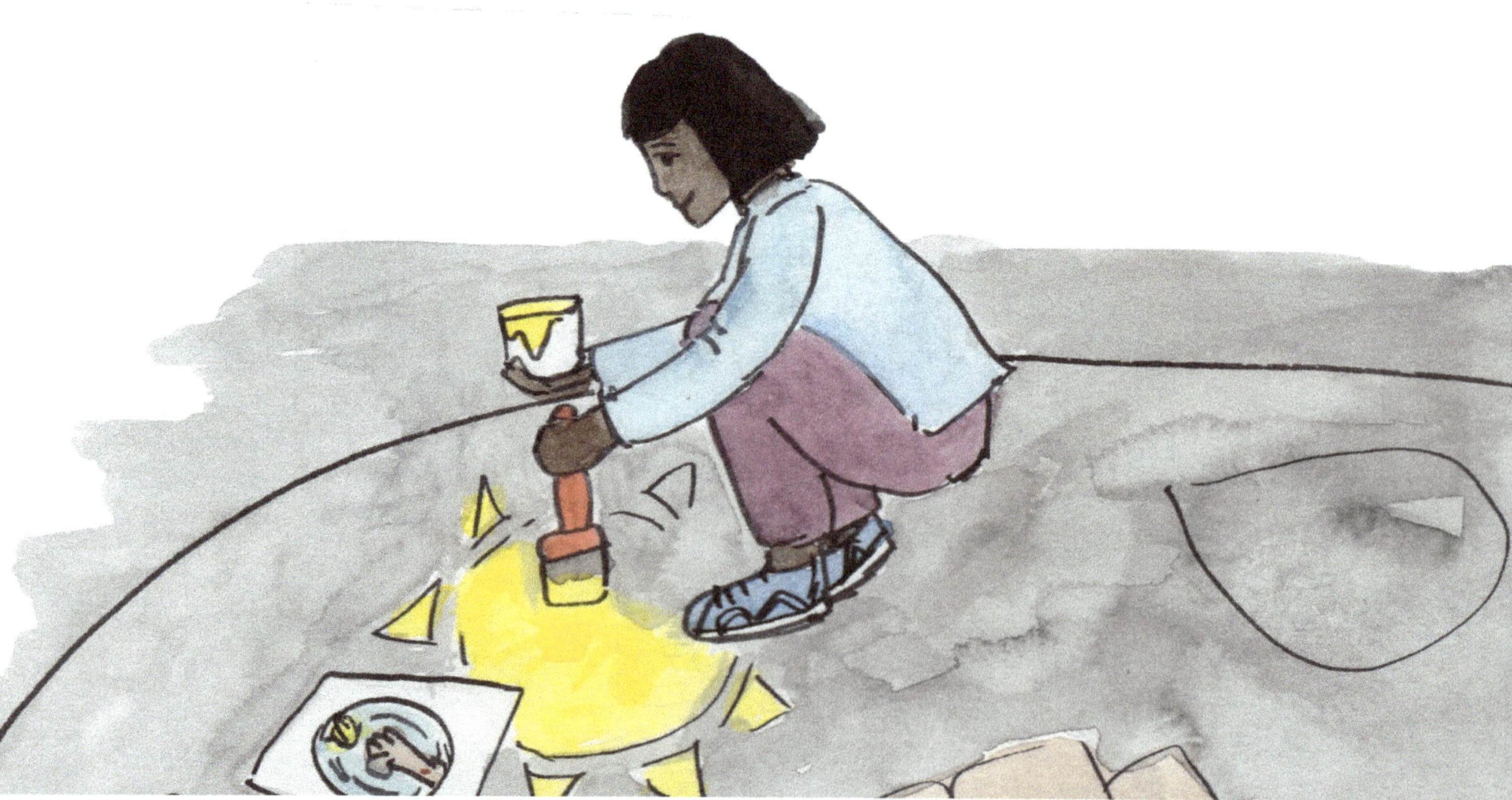

HOW TO MAKE STENCILS

Stencils are great for reproducing images or text. They are easy and cheap to make, they can be used on a variety of surfaces and you can produce many images from a single stencil.

You can stencil onto..

- **Clothing**
  Such as shirts, jackets, vests, etc. You can make matching shirts for a group or event.

- **Posters**
  You can use stencils to make posters - just keep it simple!

- **Banners**
  Stencil onto fabric to make lots of small banners. This is a great way to have a visually unified presence at an event. (Remember you can easily dye fabric with house paint and water.)

- **Flags**
  You can stencil an image for crossbar flags or other types of flags.

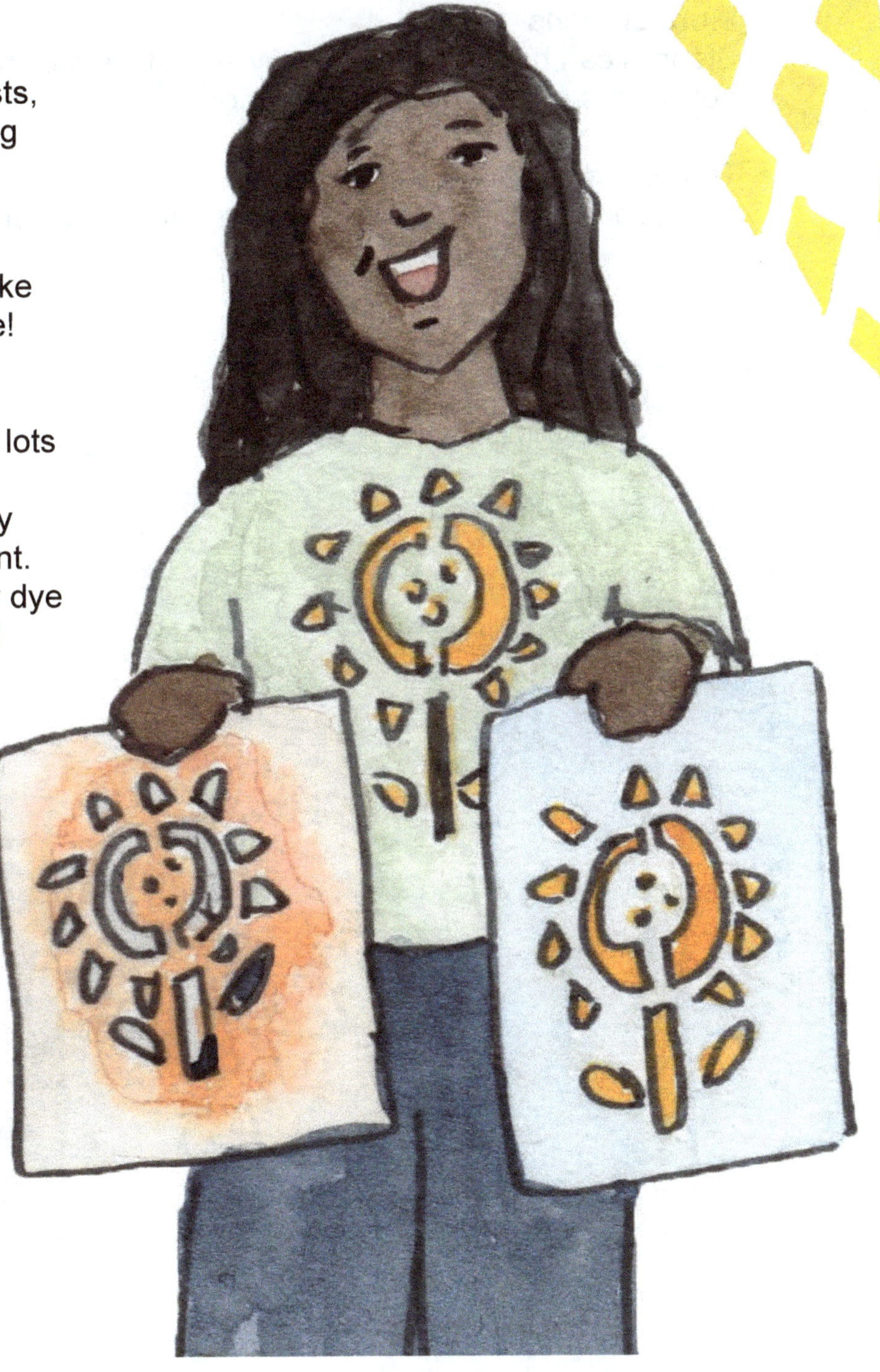

- **Placards**
  Make cardboard signs and print your stencil onto the sign to carry at an event

- **Buildings**
  A.k.a. street art! Putting your message into public spaces is a great way to get it seen. Doing this also reclaims the concept of public space by making it participatory and interactive -- a model for what other societies are possible. You can also stencil on paper (like a poster) and wheat-paste the posters up.

- **Patches or armbands**
  Stencil onto small pieces of fabric and sew or tie on.

- **More stencils**
  Stencils can be reproduced easily -- just stencil onto good material then cut it out. This is especially good if your original stencil gets worn out.

- **Tote bags…. and more!**
  Stencilled clothing, bags and patches are great items to sell for fundraisers!

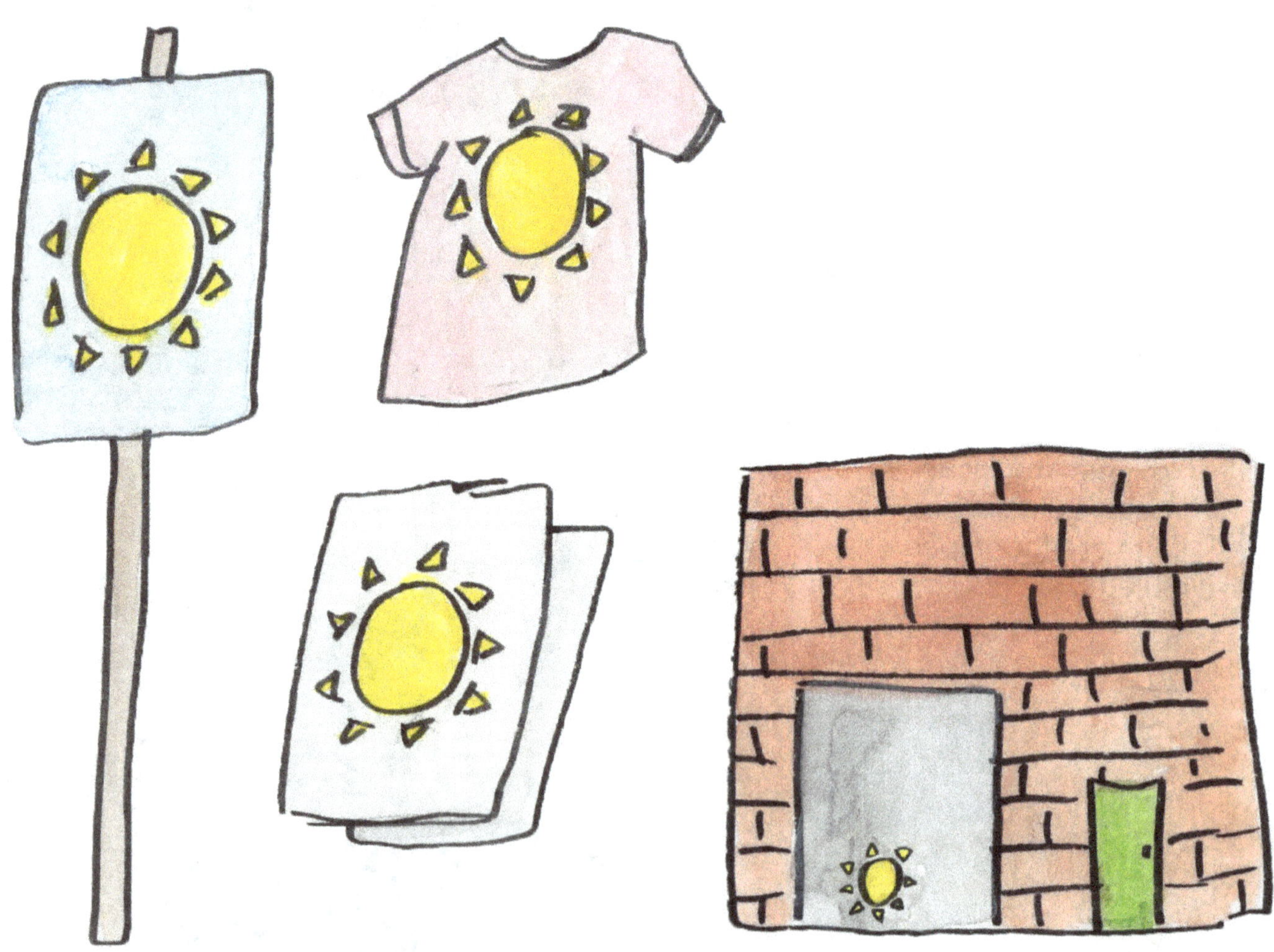

STEP ONE: GATHER SUPPLIES

- **Thin cardboard or thin plastic** such as mylar, acetate sheets, or any water-resistant heavy paper. Cereal-box weight cardboard works well.
- **Spray paint or acrylic or latex paint**
- **Mask and gloves** (for safe spray painting)
- **Rollers or sponges** (if not using spray paint) Rollers are faster, but sponges also work
- **Utility knife and extra blades** (have many of these if many people are making stencils)
- **Cutting mat** (to use with utility knife. Have many of these if many people are making stencils)
- **Surfaces to stencil onto** such as fabric, paper or signs
- **Thin wire** (to reinforce bridges, and also bring wire cutters)
- **Pencils, sharpies and scrap paper**
- **Rags**
- **Drop cloth(s)**
- **Ruler(s)**
- **Adhesive** (such as repositionable spray adhesive or painters' tape. Don't get heavy duty permanent spray adhesive!)
- **Stabilizer** (optional but can be useful) such as a stick, dowel or pencil
- **Scrap material** (to test print onto such as newsprint, extra cardboard....)

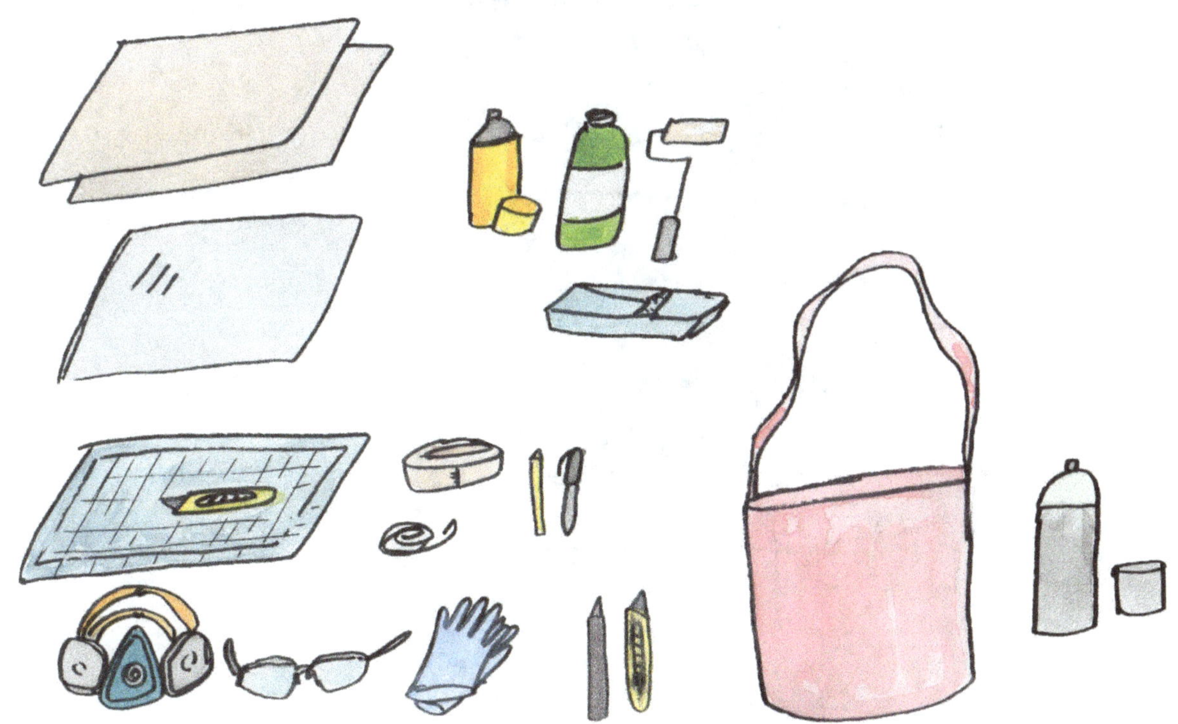

STEP TWO: CHOOSE OR DESIGN AN IMAGE

First you need to choose or design an image.

- You can use an existing image from 350 or other organizations, you can commission an artist in the community to design some images for your group to use, or you can design your own image.

- In any case think about the message you want to share through image and/or text and choose, commission or develop accordingly! If you are designing your own start with some sketches.

- Stencils could range from simple to complex and anywhere in between, but starting off simple helps to get the hang of it.

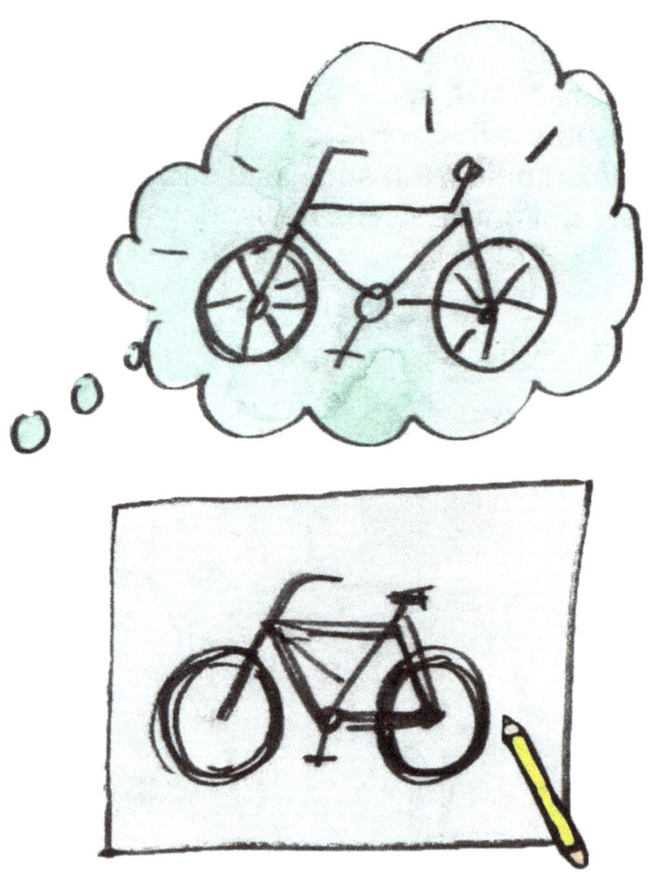

Next turn your sketch into a stencil design

- If you are creating a design, remember:

  - When designing a stencil image (as with most design) you are working
    with two elements - **negative space** and **positive space**. The negative
    space is space around an object/image (i.e., background) and positive
    space is the object or image.

  - For a basic stencil you will create a two-color design. You cut your
    positive space out of your stencil material and these areas will be the
    color of the paint. Whatever you leave covered by the stencil (negative
    space) is your surface color that you are stenciling onto.

  - In your design make sure there are no negative spaces (what stays) fully
    surrounded by positive space (what you cut away). The positive spaces
    which could completely close, eliminating negative space inside of them,
    are called **islands** - such as the middle of an A, O, B, etc. Your islands
    need to be attached by '**bridges**' to another section of negative space.
    - If you have thin bridges you can reinforce them by taping wire to
      them.

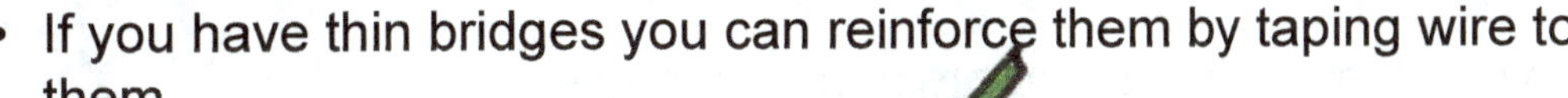

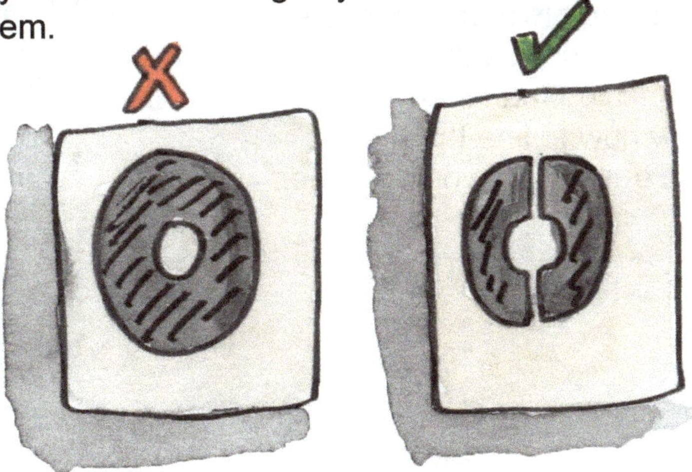

A FEW MORE DESIGN TIPS..

- It can be helpful to look up 'stencil design' or 'stencil template' online for ideas, to see how others have designed images, and to see the way that the negative and positive space works.

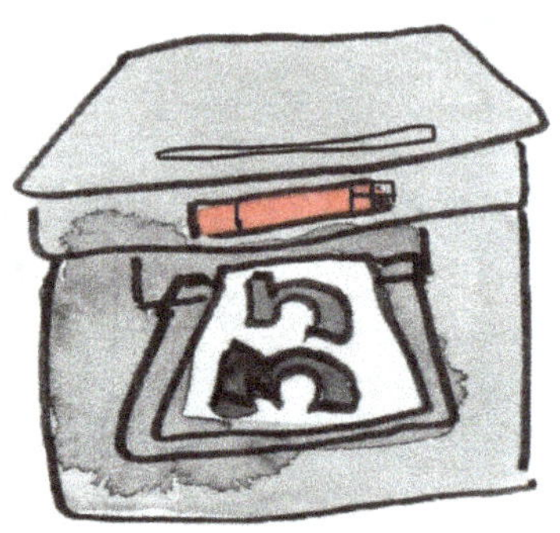

- You can create your design by hand or on the computer.
    - With a digital image you could then print it or project it to transfer it to your stencil material.
    - If you print an image you can glue it to your stencil paper and cut through both layers together.
    - You can trace it on if you are using a clear surface such as mylar or acetate, or if you get enough light coming, through you can hold it up to a window to trace.

- Another good way to transfer images onto your stencil material is to cut your design out on paper first (either your drawn design or a printed design), and then paint or trace the image onto your sturdy stencil material from your paper 'stencil'. This way you can also make sure there no islands.

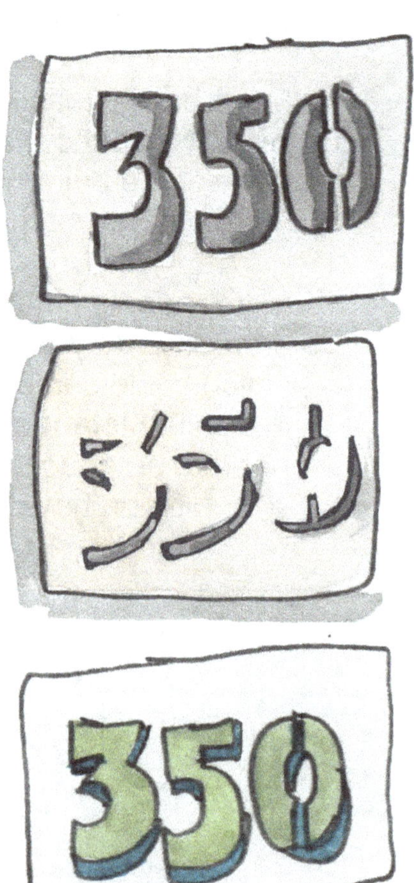

- If you want additional colors, you can make a multi-layer image. Each color will need its own stencil. Put matching marks on each stencil so you know how to line them up easily and plan the designs to work together.

STEP THREE: CUT OUT YOUR STENCIL

- Cut with the utility knife on a cutting mat. It can be helpful to turn the stencil to make cuts at a comfortable angle rather than manipulating the knife in odd ways.

  ** Keep your fingers safe by keeping them away from the blade and always cutting directionally away from your fingers. **

- Sharper blades cut better, so have extra blades, and don't hesitate to switch when one gets dull.

- Discard the sharp blades safely (i.e., wrapped in cardboard and tape, or in a taped container and labelled 'sharps').

- If you discover you had an island without a bridge (after you have cut it), don't fret, you can re-attach it with a wire or cardboard bridge taped to the back of the stencil.

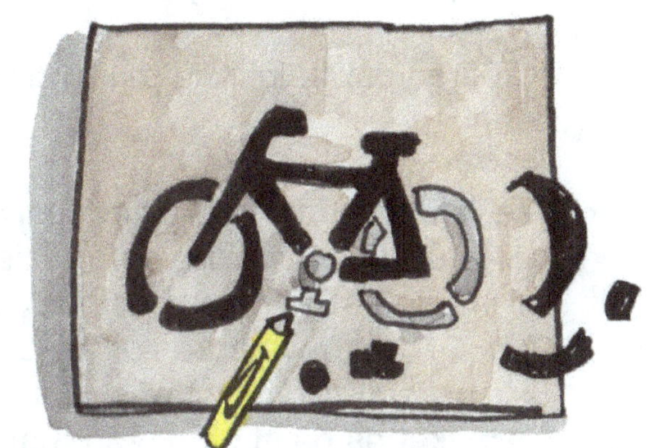

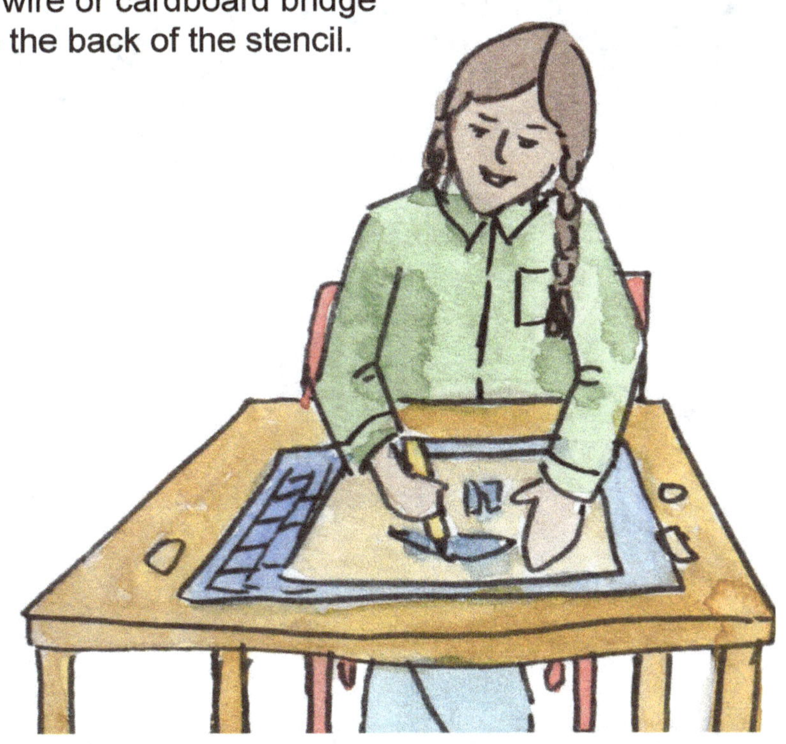

STEP FOUR: PRINT YOUR STENCIL

Now it's time to put your stencil to use! Use a roller or spray paint.

- Get whatever you are planning to print on ready. Have scrap paper ready to do a test print on before you go ahead with all your printing.

- Prepare your paint and painting space. Lay drop cloths to keep the table or floor clean.

- Use repositionable spray adhesive or tape to secure your stencil to the surface that you will be printing onto. This is to keep the stencil from moving to make the image as crisp as possible.
    - If you have areas of the stencil that are sticking up, you can use the stabilizer pencil or stick to hold that area down. Using a pencil or stick keeps paint off of your hands.

- Tip for t-shirts:
    - Put a piece of cardboard inside so the paint doesn't bleed through the front of the shirt to the back, or vice versa. Latex paint works great with normal t-shirts. Spray paint can be used with thin and light coloured fabric. You can also get fabric paints from art or craft stores.

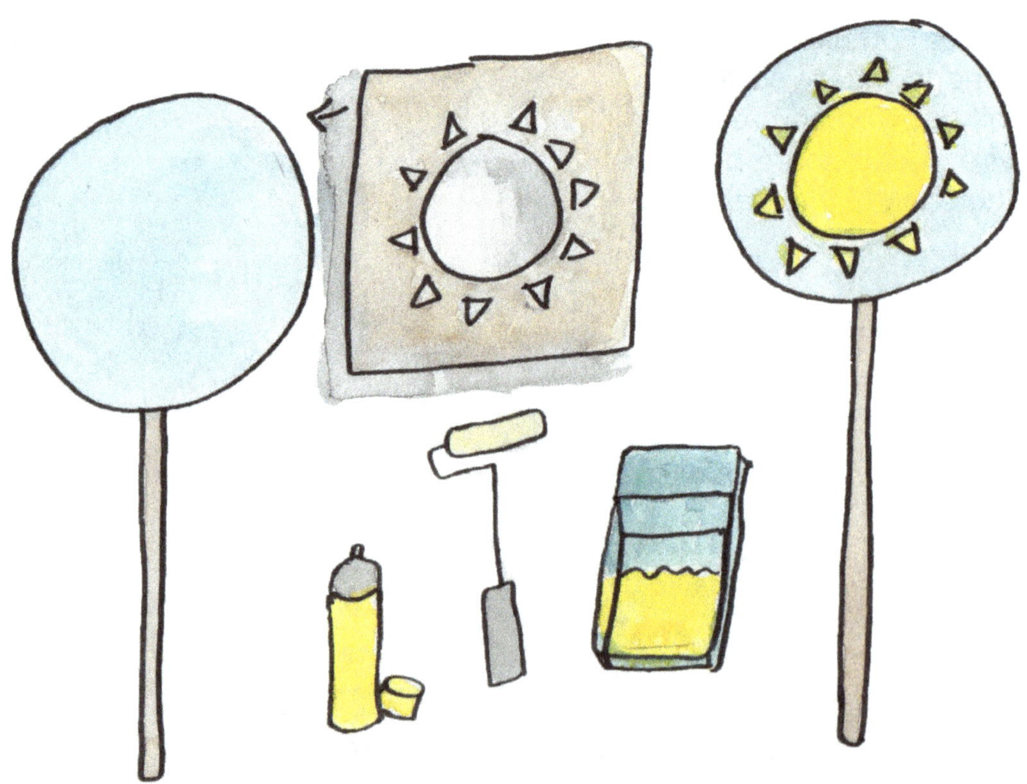

Spray painting a stencil

- Spray paint works well if you need to be quick, or if you are working on a rough surface. It tends to leave the crispest image, but it is more expensive and more toxic than house paint.

- Use spray paint outdoors and wear a mask and gloves.

- Follow the instructions on the can – shake before use. When you are done for the day, spray upside down to empty the nozzle.

- Spray in short strokes with the can held horizontally. Don't angle the spray can to avoid pointing underneath the edges of the stencil.

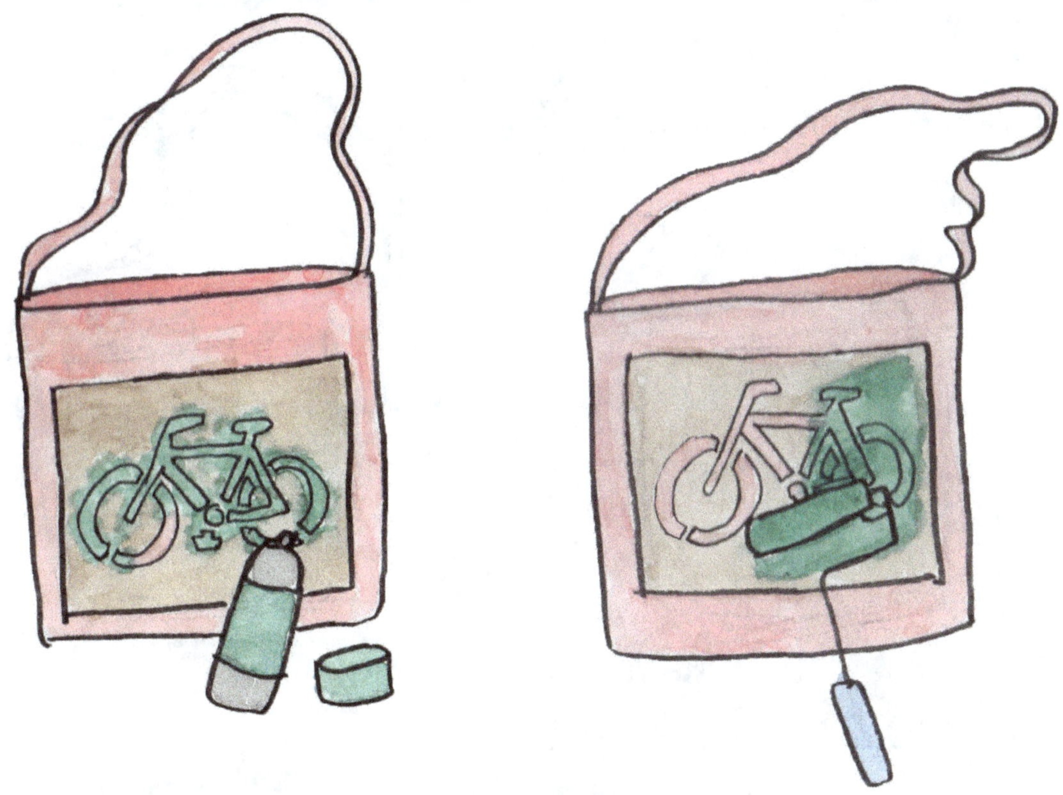

Using Latex house paint or acrylic paint with a roller or sponge

- Pour the paint into a paint tray and roll or dab the sponge with paint from there.

- The trick is to get just the right amount of paint on the roller (or brush or sponge) you are using. Do a few practices on cardboard or scrap paper.

- Aim for a medium thick and even coat. Thick paint can glob underneath the stencil. If your paint tray is small, or you don't have one, you can also roll your paint out on a paint palette or a piece of cardboard before rolling over the stencil.

- When printing many of the same stencil, wipe the stencil off extra paint or let it dry when the image stops being crisp. Never put anything on top of a wet (or even damp) stencil, or it will stick and rip the stencil.

- If you spray-painted an image for posters or flags, you (or others) can add hand painted elements of the images after they are printed. This is also a great way for a group of volunteers or event attendees to add a personal touch onto a unified visual.

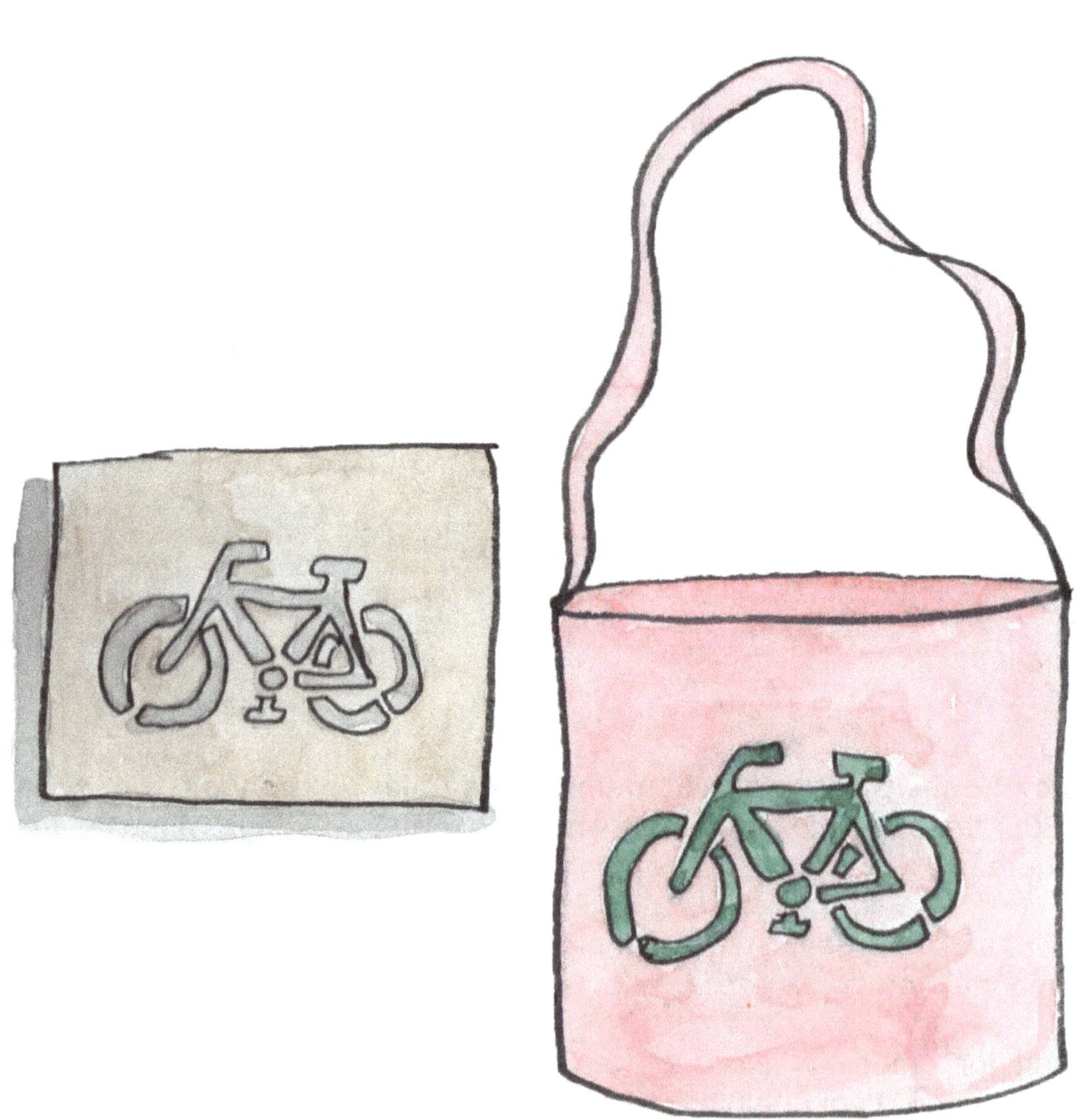

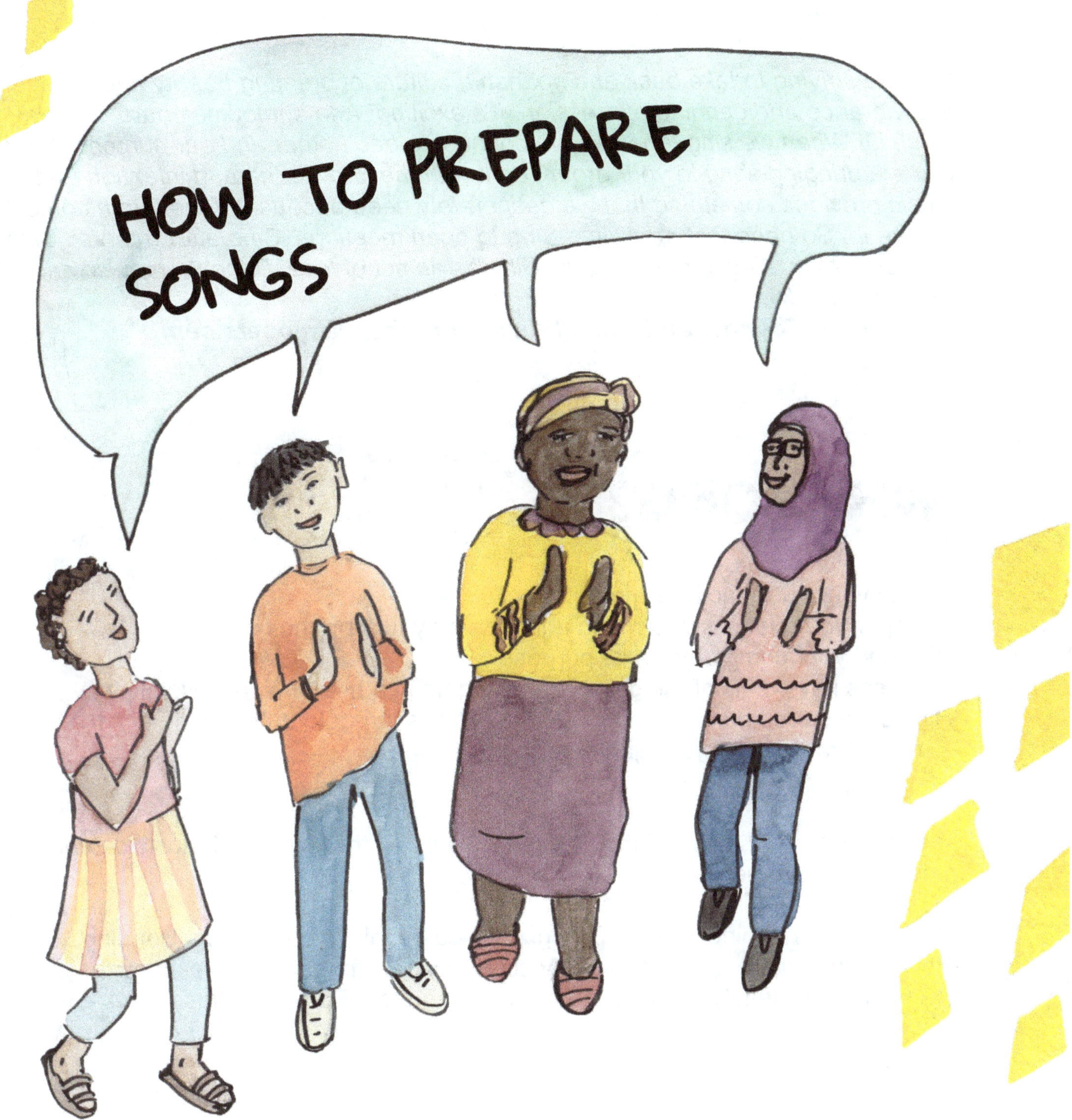

"Singing is another important connective practice. Songs unify us in ways that can feel mysterious, magical and sometimes even spiritual. Songs help us stay calm and resolute during a demonstration; channel anger, sadness or grief; raise each other's spirits; and share history, heritage, and culture with one another." - Sara Blazevic and Aru Shiney-Ajay (p. 166 in *Winning the Green New Deal*)

"We are striving to take back and nourish a culture of creating beauty and color and vibrance and genuine expression. It's exciting! And sometimes hard. But it's worth it!! When we sing together, we connect to each other and our purpose. So if you are bringing song to your group, do it with the knowledge and intention that music provides something that we desperately need because of the harsh context we live in. So bring that medicine. Sing to open meetings. Sing after a break. Sing to open a rally. Sing to close a vigil. Sing as an act of love. Bring that music and let it elevate us all."
-Lu Aya, Co-Founder and Artist Educator of thepeacepoets.com

WHY SONG?

• Make your public actions more impactful
• Deepen the relationships within and beyond your community
• Ground your community in its purpose
• Express key points of the group's messaging in a beautiful, accessible way
• Unveil the deep human emotion of the group's struggle to the world
• Bring vibrancy to all your gatherings

This is a list from Lu Aya of the Peace Poets on all the ways that music can be a part of the movement:

Gathering, Grounding, Focus, Energizing, De-escalation, Grieving, Bonding, Moving, Transitioning, Escalating, Accompanying, Channeling, Messaging, Transforming, Beauty, Rage, Love, Connectedness, Purpose, Closing

WHEN TO BRING IN SONG

• Opening or closing a meeting
• At Town Hall Meetings
• At public events, actions, or rallies
• Anywhere else that you want!

WHERE TO FIND SONGS

There are many amazing writers who have created movements songs.
- You can look online for 'climate justice songs' and often find videos of them being performed as well.
- You can write your own lyrics to a common tune.

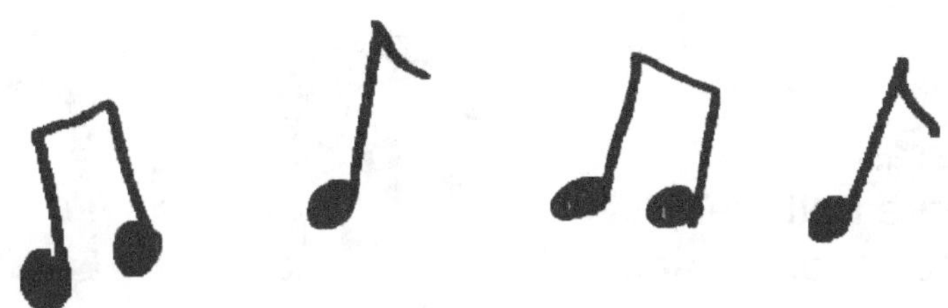

TIPS FOR SONG LEADING

- **Before** - practice alone and leading others.
- **Share** - lead your friends, family and others in the song.
- **Brainstorm** - the words you can add to the song to improvise with.
- **Know content** - of the event before and after song so you know the tone.
- **Build it in** - plan song into the program and schedule.
- **Story** - learn and reflect on the testimonies of struggle your song speaks to.
- **Connect** - feel the song connect you to history, purpose and comrades.
- **Window** - find the specific parts of your song where you can interject phrases like "sing it loud", "for your neighbors", "dance with it", etc. (sometimes this will need to be over the singing).
- **Tempo** - make a chill song energizing or vice versa.
- **Volume** - utilize volume to manage the tone and vibe of the group ("let's get loud!" vs. "sing it gently now").

As a final note, remember to bring a megaphone or have a sound system set up if you need to, to make sure that the song leader can be heard. Depending on the event or location you can project lyrics or hand out printed sheets with lyrics to help people learn the song or join in!

HOW TO TAKE EVENT PHOTOGRAPHS

Capture the energy and message of the event using a variety of shots, media, and platforms. This helps to share the event and increase its impact!

Supplies
- DSLR Camera
- Smart phones' cameras
- If available, pack spare batteries, battery packs for smartphones, and wifi-dongles!
- Tripod (optional)

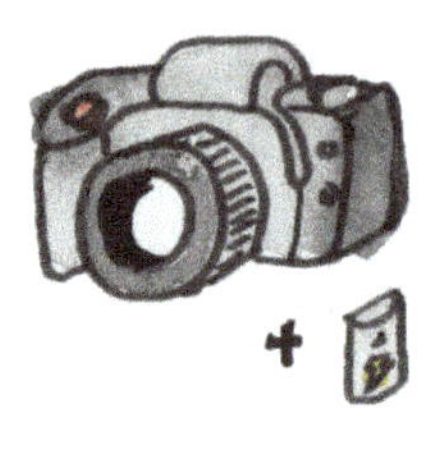
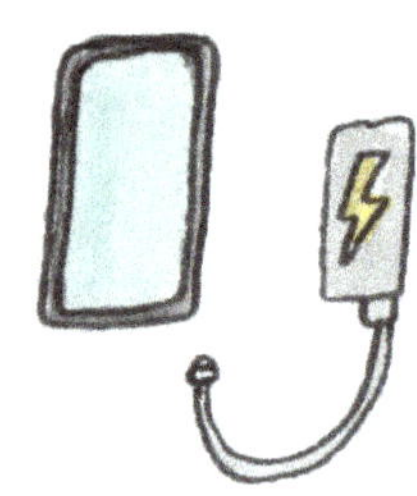
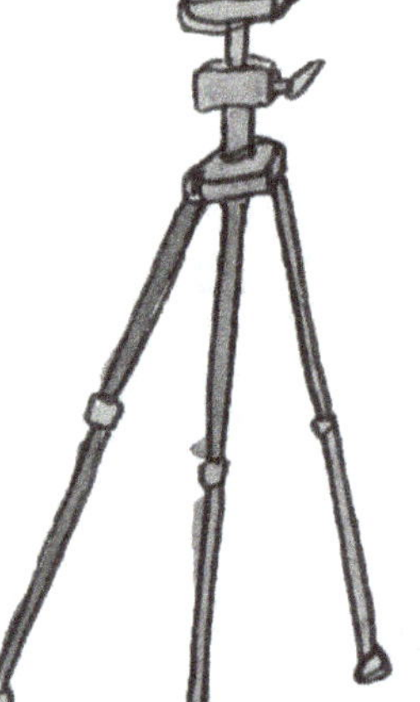
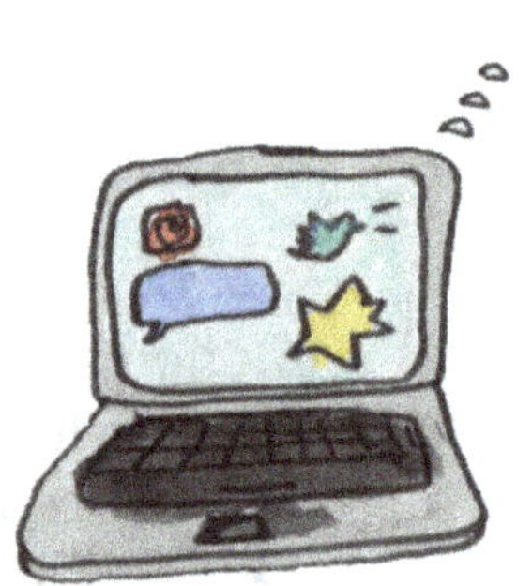
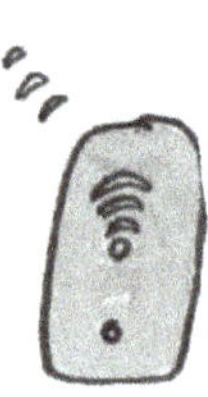

Photographer
Have at least one person (more if the event is larger) as a dedicated photographer.

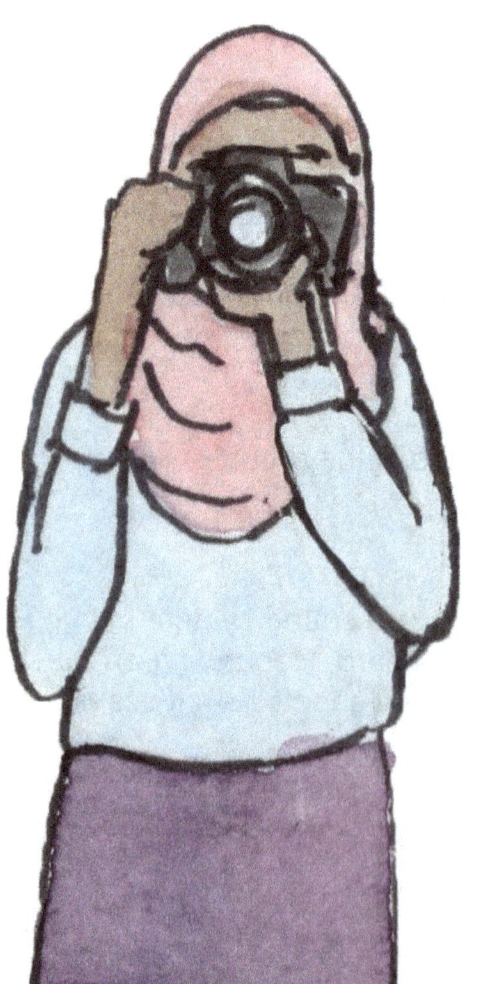

Reminder:
As a photographer, how you interact at an action makes a big difference. Connect with people. Smile. When there is time/opportunity, it can help to talk to people first, introduce yourself, ask their story, be seen interacting with the organizers, so folks know you're on their side. This is especially true if you are an outsider of some sort (e.g., different nationality, language, community, etc.). Be respectful of people's boundaries, especially around photographing children, prayer, ceremony, etc. Ask if photo/video is appropriate.

TAKING PHOTOS

Take lots of photos all through the event. Take more than one shot of your subject. This will allow you a choice from which you can select your best images. Be creative with some of your shots!

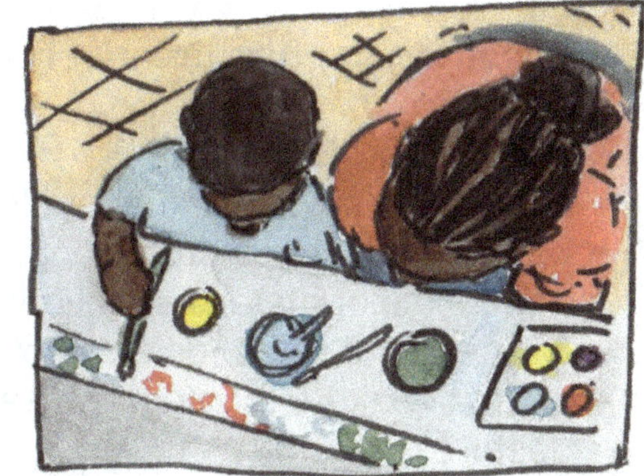

Try different angles. People are used to seeing the world at eye level, so try moving to different positions to see your subject at different angles. Crouch down, move left or right. Photos from far away, high up, or middle shots also provide important variety.

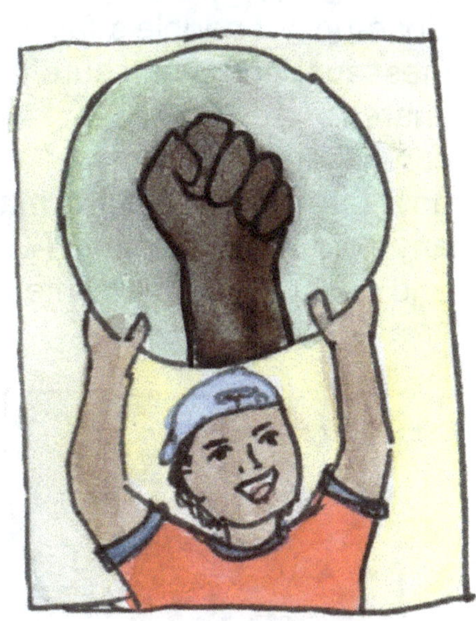

Share the story by capturing main messages on banners and signs in your photos. Include signage that shows name of target (e.g., sign on a building). Photos of poignant signs, clear messages and important landmarks provide context. If you have multiple cameras you can set one up on a tripod for the duration of an event and do a time lapse.

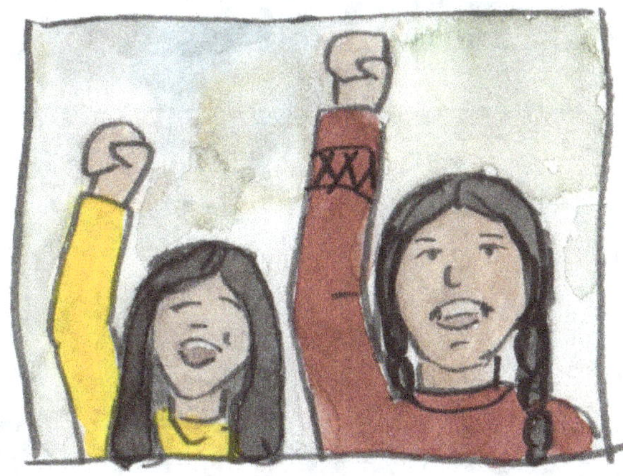

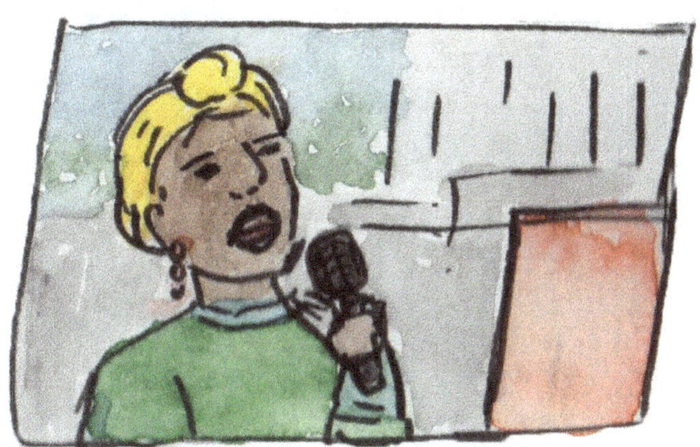

CAPTURE A VARIETY OF SHOTS

You want to capture creatively different scenes, moments and people!

Take photos of:
- set-up, people signing in, putting on stickers/buttons,
- behind-the-scenes organizing,
- pamphlets or materials laid out,
- banners and signs (diversity of people holding them),
- event speakers (photograph each speaker and catch their emotions and gestures),
- people clapping, cheering, smiling, chanting, fists raised,
- people being hopeful, energetic, determined,
- posed group shots (more on that below!!),
- close-ups of people's faces, feet or hands (capture personality as well as the message, and make sure that they consent to having their photo taken and shared),
- crowds at their largest,
- any "targets" or decision makers,
- any notable participants (who are adding clout to your action),
- and event participants interacting with passersby.

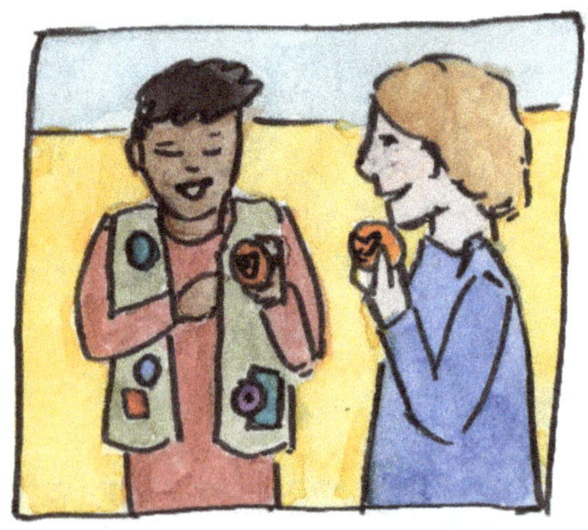

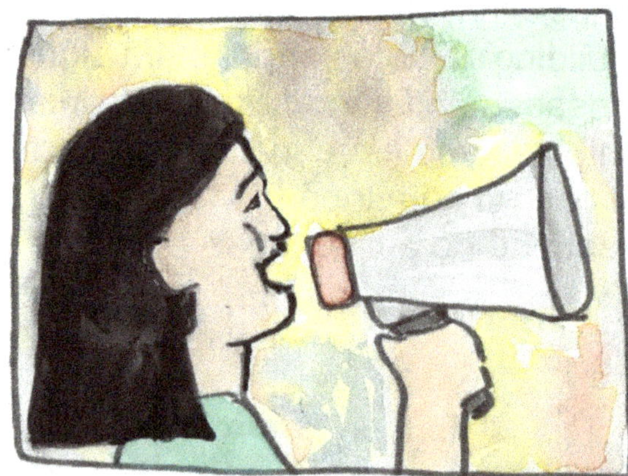

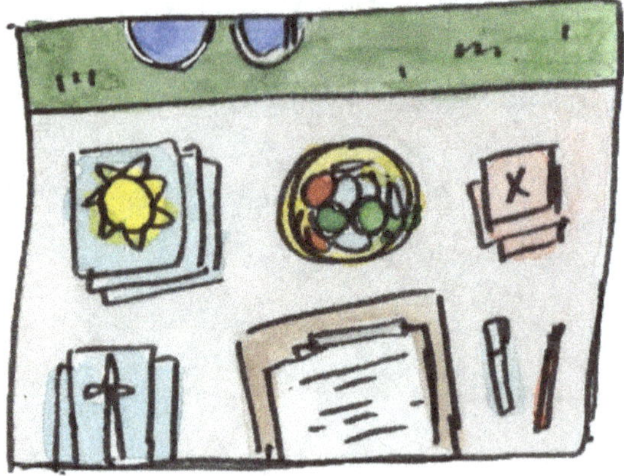

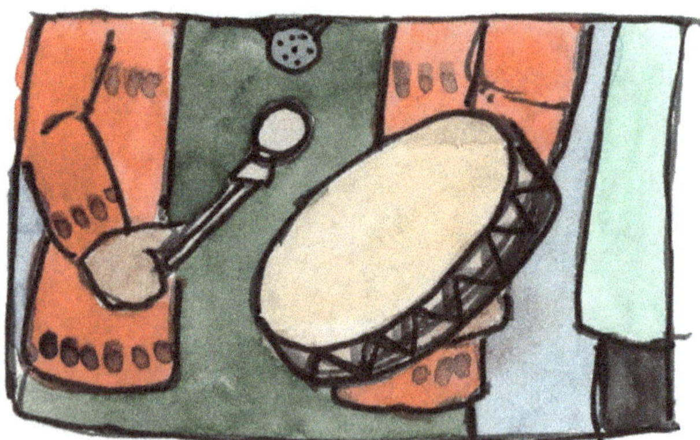

GROUP PHOTO

Getting a group photo of everyone with all the signs, art and visuals can capture an impactful image of the demonstration or event. Here are a few tips for a strong group photo.

Plan your group photo
Make time in your runsheet for LOTS of posed group photos. Take as many as you can, so you have lots of photos to choose from. Try different angles, distances, group positions, etc. Take the group photo before people start to leave!

Photographer:
Have someone reliable (e.g., your event photographer) ready to take the photo. If you know media photographers or videographers are coming, you could let them know there will be a group photo at a certain time/location.

Timing:
Time your group photo for when the most people are present. This may be in the middle of your event.

Perform an action
Ask everyone to perform the same action when the photo is taken! You could try arranging your arms in the Fossil Free cross, lift up a fist in resistance, wave signs in the air, or get a photo of each of these actions. It can be helpful to have an MC or organizer direct the group if the group is large.

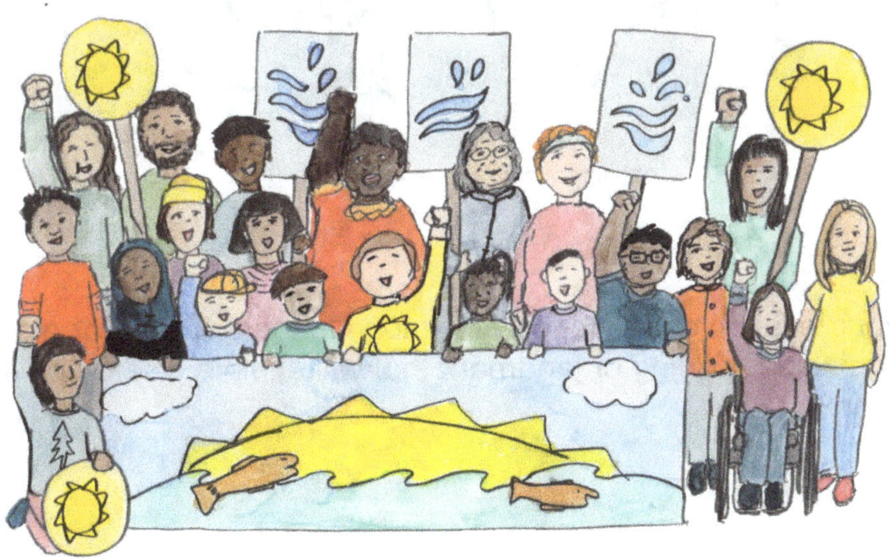

Framing

Make sure your photo is tight and centered on the group of people you are taking a photo of. Don't leave lots of empty space around the sides, unless it's an important backdrop. Take at least one landscape and one portrait photo.

Lighting

Pay attention to where the light is coming from. If the sun is out, have the group to the side of the sun or facing the sun. Having the sun behind the group can make them back-lit (with their faces in shadow).
If it's dusk or dark, look for street lights or other sources of light–again ideally coming in front of the group, not behind them.

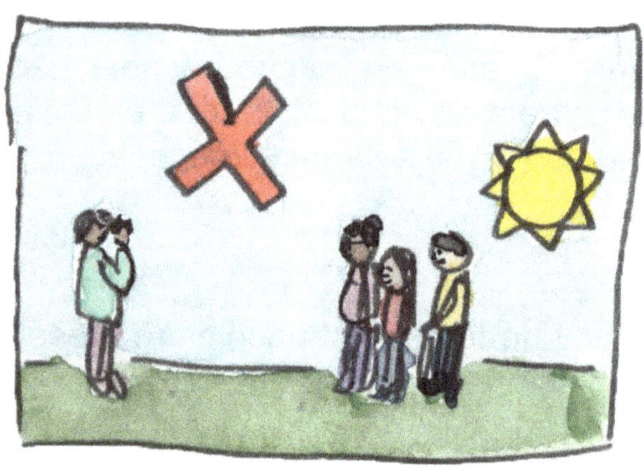

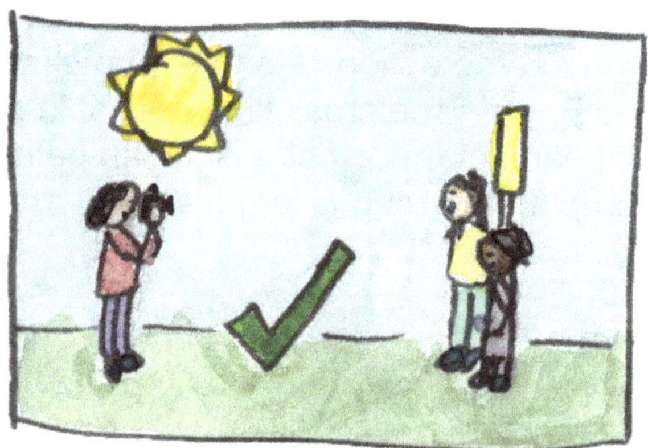

Backdrop

Consider how your location can help tell your story. Is there a sign for a politician's office, or a recognizable building or landmark that will explain where you are and help to tell the story?

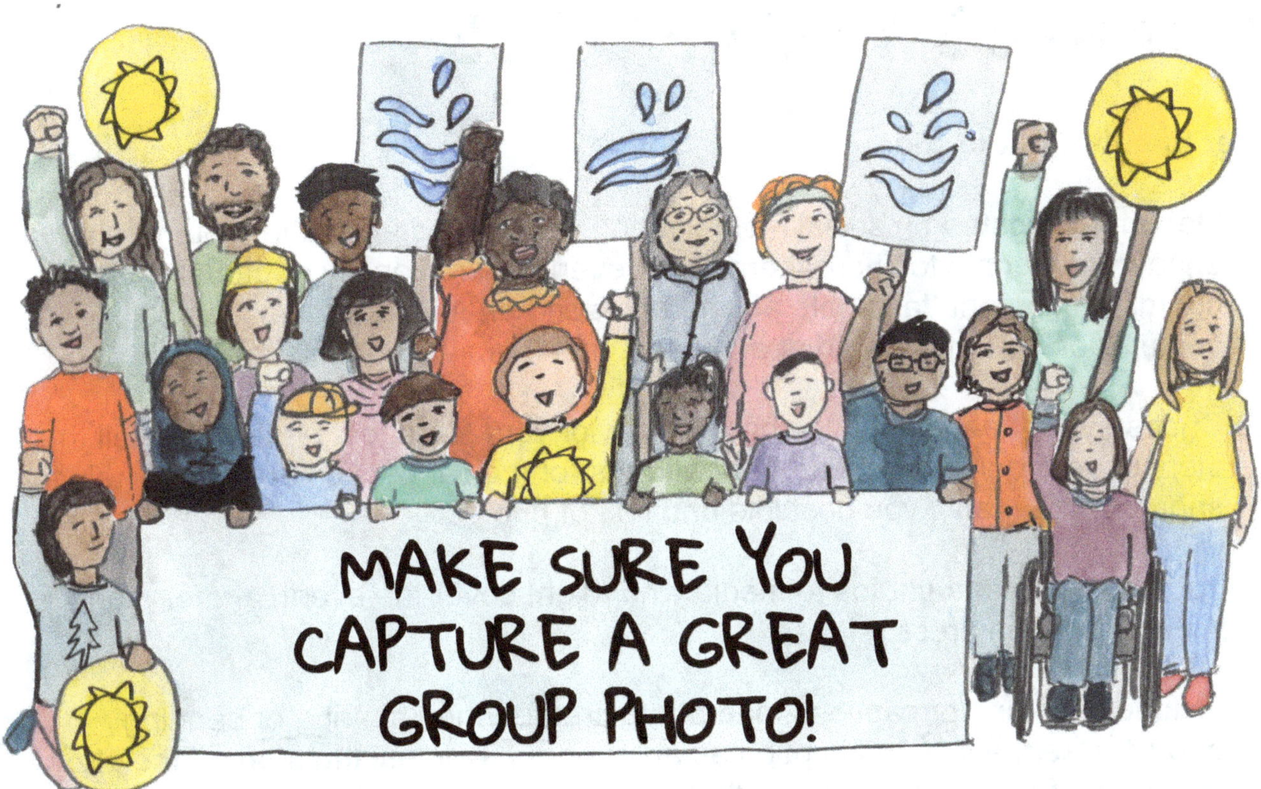

Vertical layering

Try to arrange people and art so they are all visible. You can do this through vertical layering, so ask people to:

- fill the space and don't block each other,
- have tall people in the back row and less tall people in front,
- have the front row of people sitting on the ground if that works for them,
- have a second row of folks kneeling,
- have some people stand on steps, benches, walls if they can, so they can be seen behind those standing on the ground,
- make sure everyone can see the photographer clearly -- check and make sure their faces will be included in the photo.

Art and visuals

Are there strong readable key banner(s) or sign(s) that state your core message? Put these in the center of the group photo. This is the time to arrange your strongest art and visuals to be seen, to make your group bigger and your message clear and beautiful. Ask people with signs to hold them either high or low enough that they don't block other faces. For example, cross-bar flags can be held in the back row above everyone's heads, and additional banners can be laid flat on the ground in front of the group and included in the photo frame.

SHARING THE PHOTOS

Get the photos out there

- Get photos posted on social media during and immediately after your event, and encourage people to share them. If the event is a nationally or globally coordinated event, take note of where to send photos for national/global compilation. Also take note of and use event hashtags when sharing.

- Choose your best photos to share. A few of your strongest photos that tell the story of your demonstration/event with a strong clear caption are more likely to shared more than if you post lots and lots of photos.

- You can also send photos to media who might cover the event, and/or along with a follow-up press release.

- Include titles and/or captions, and photo credits when sharing or sending photos. Use the title and caption as an opportunity to tell the story of the photo, give a bit of context and tie together elements in the image for the viewer.

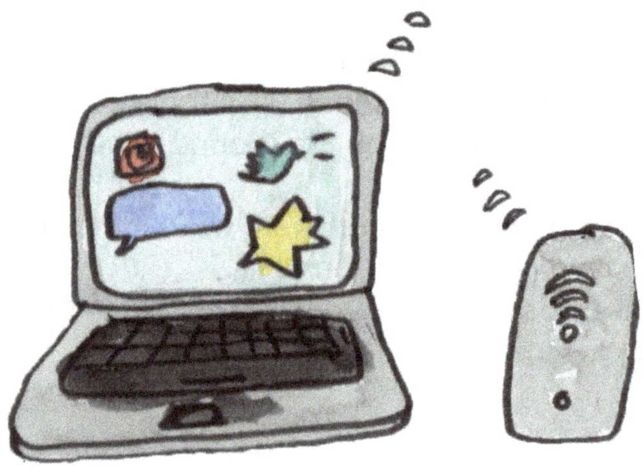

While this info is geared towards event and action photography, remember that it is also great to get photos of the behind-the-scenes, everyday activities, or smaller events such as meetings, workshops, art builds or canvassing. These can be used for social media, slideshows or other general uses!

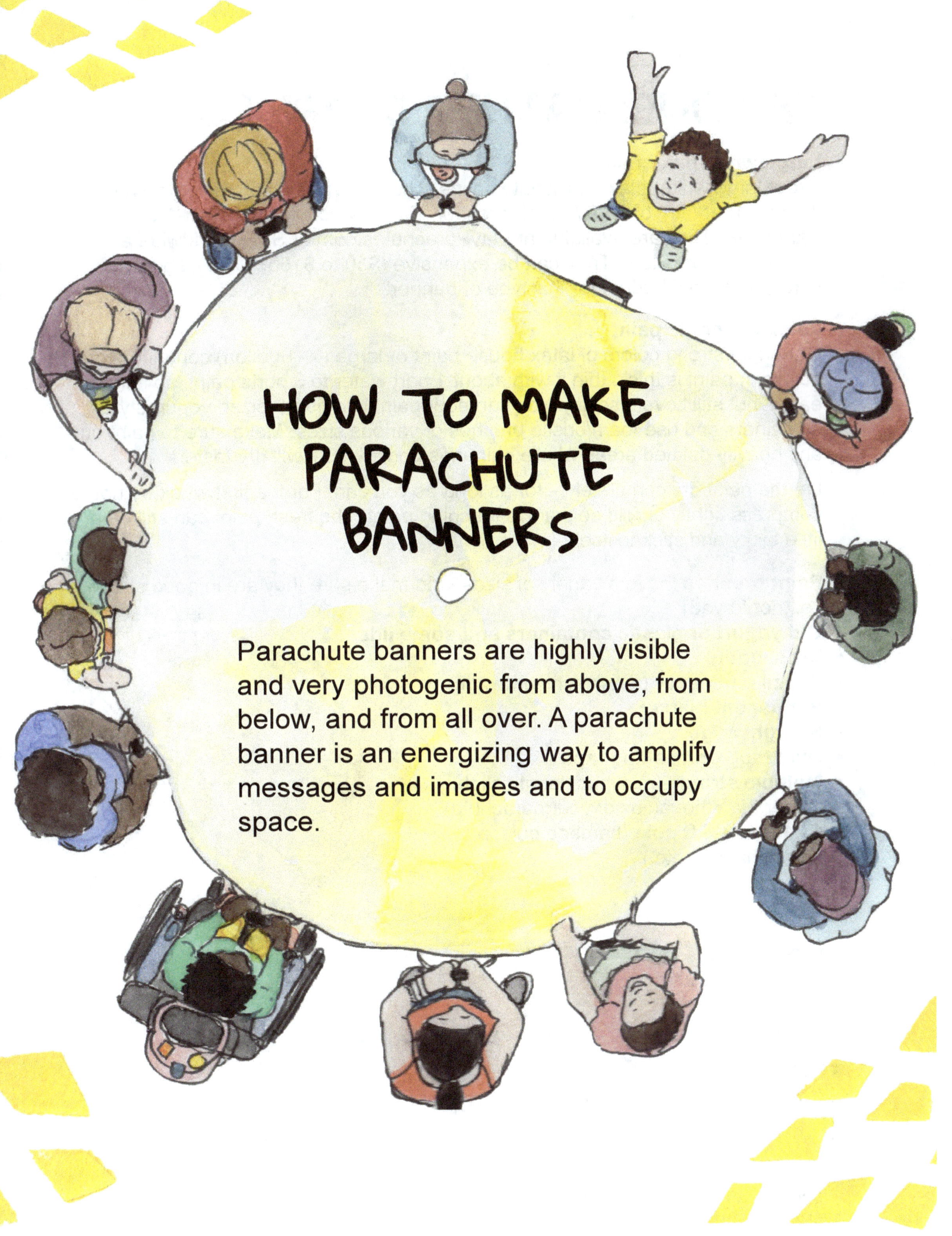

HOW TO MAKE PARACHUTE BANNERS

Parachute banners are highly visible and very photogenic from above, from below, and from all over. A parachute banner is an energizing way to amplify messages and images and to occupy space.

STEP ONE: GATHER SUPPLIES

- **Large white parachute**
  Order large white "play" parachute online. There are a few common sizes (12 ft/3.5m, 16 ft /5m or 24 ft /7m. Search for "Play Parachute" or "Color-Me Parachute" They are available at PlayParachutes.com or S&S Worldwide as well as other retailers. They can be expensive ($50 to $150+ USD), so make sure you have a budget for this type of banner!

- **Latex or acrylic paint**
  Get bright strong colors of latex house paint or large (½-1 gallon) containers of acrylic. If paint is thick, thin it with about 1 part water to 3 parts paint, so it flows easily, but still covers solidly. You can pour paint into quart- sized yogurt style containers and use foam/bristle brushes of various sizes. Make sure to paint out any heavily painted areas where paint has pooled, so it will dry faster.

  Let the paint dry completely – for as long as you can. For the first week try not to compress tightly or fold so paint is touching paint. The fresh paint can still be a little tacky and stick to itself.

- **Paint brushes** (have a variety of sizes, and make sure they are in good shape, i.e., not frayed)
- **Old yogurt or plastic containers and some lids**
- **Drop cloths**
- **Pencil and paper** (for sketching design)
- **Permanent marker**
- **Straight edge**
- **Duct tape or masking tape**
- **Multiple strings** (minimum length slightly longer than the radius of your parachute)
- **1 - 1.5 m/3-5 ft pole** (bamboo pole, a broom handle, etc.)

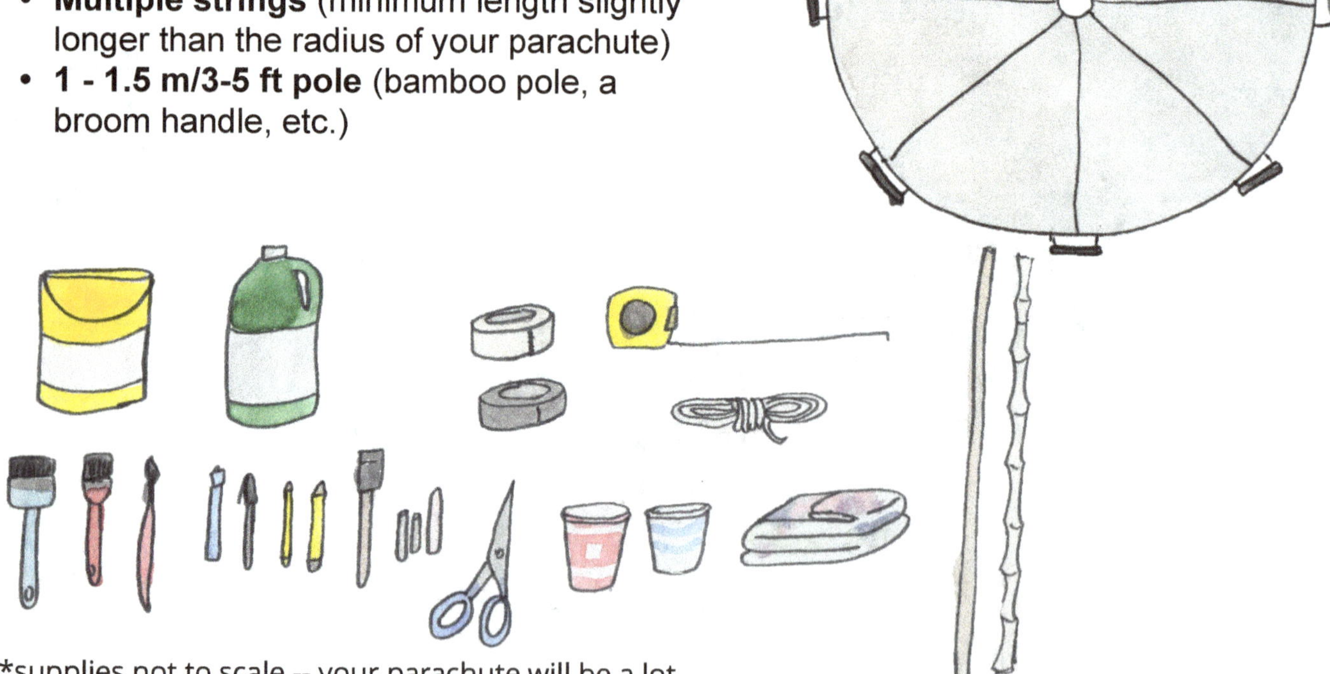

*supplies not to scale -- your parachute will be a lot bigger in comparison to the rest of the supplies!

STEP TWO: DESIGN

Decide — What few words and what simple, clear image(s) communicate some of your core message or story? What colors?

Tips:
- **Keep it simple** - the more complex the image and the more/longer words you choose, the longer it takes to lay out and paint. Many of the parachute photos in media coverage are taken from below, with light shining through like stained glass windows, whether or not the words and images are clear.
- **High contrast** - between the background and the text colors!
- **Circle layout** - Laying out a design and text in a circle or arc works well, but you can also have your text run horizontal.
- **Look at examples** - search "parachute climate" or "parachute protest" online to see other designs and how they were photographed in the media.

STEP THREE: FIND SPACE

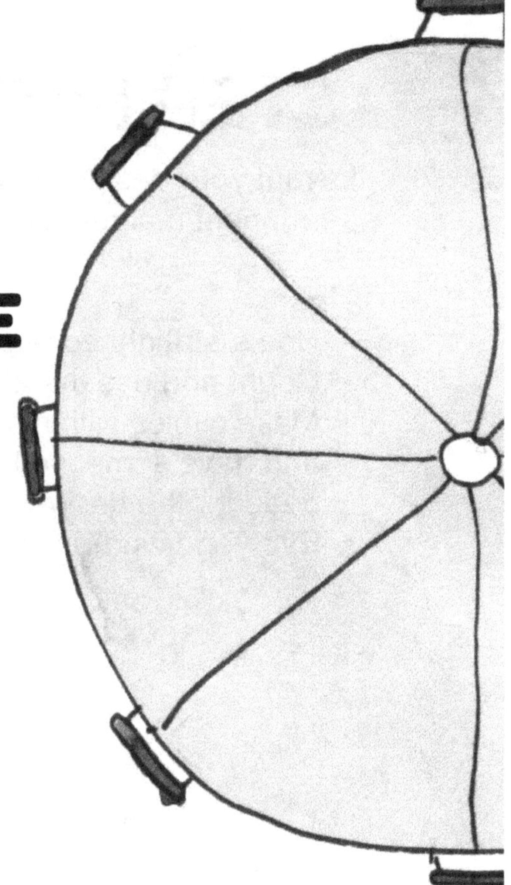

You'll need a space big enough to lay your entire parachute out flat. Get a flat, ideally smooth, place to lay it out and paint it. There needs to be flat space at least the size of the parachute laid out. If your parachute is 24'x'24'/ 7m x 7m, that's a pretty big space. You may have to find an outdoor space.

- Some possibilities include garages, gymnasiums, empty classrooms, community centers or outdoor spaces.

STEP FOUR: SPREAD THE PARACHUTE

- First lay out drop cloths (such as canvas, plastic drop cloths from paints stores or hardware stores, or old sheets) underneath your parachute because the paint will bleed through the parachute. You'll need to protect the surface you chose to work on to avoid leaving permanent artwork.

- Secure the drop cloths to the floor or ground (and to each other if there are multiple). Get duct tape (gorilla tape if taping to concrete or blacktop) or wide, high-quality masking tape (for wood or linoleum indoor floors) to tape down the drop cloths - fully stretched out– to the floor and and to each other.

- Spread out the parachute on top of the drop cloths. Then use the duct tape to tape the parachute down so it's flat without wrinkles. You can tape under each black handle, starting at two spots on opposite sides with tape at each edge.

STEP FIVE: LAYOUT THE DESIGN

Layout your design on the parachute. Sketch in pencil first and then draw using a permanent marker that is the same color of the image/paint color.

Tips:
- Use a straight edge/stick for straight lines
- Count and use the 20 parachute seams to divide up the space evenly.
- Make circles with a string compass– put a string with a loop in the exact center and have someone hold it with a marker or a stick. Then draw the circles you need for the design with a pencil at the end of the length of string.
- Everyone who is walking on the parachute should be in socks only, no shoes.

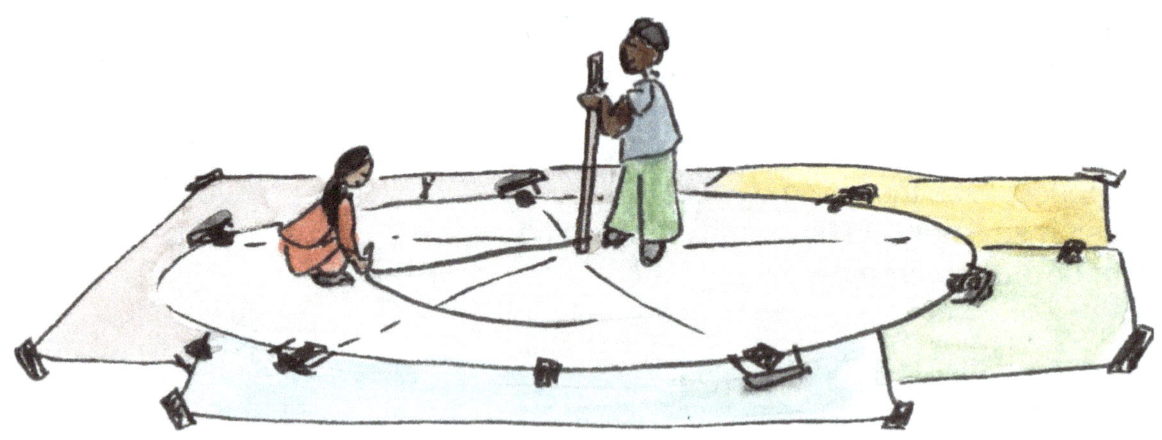

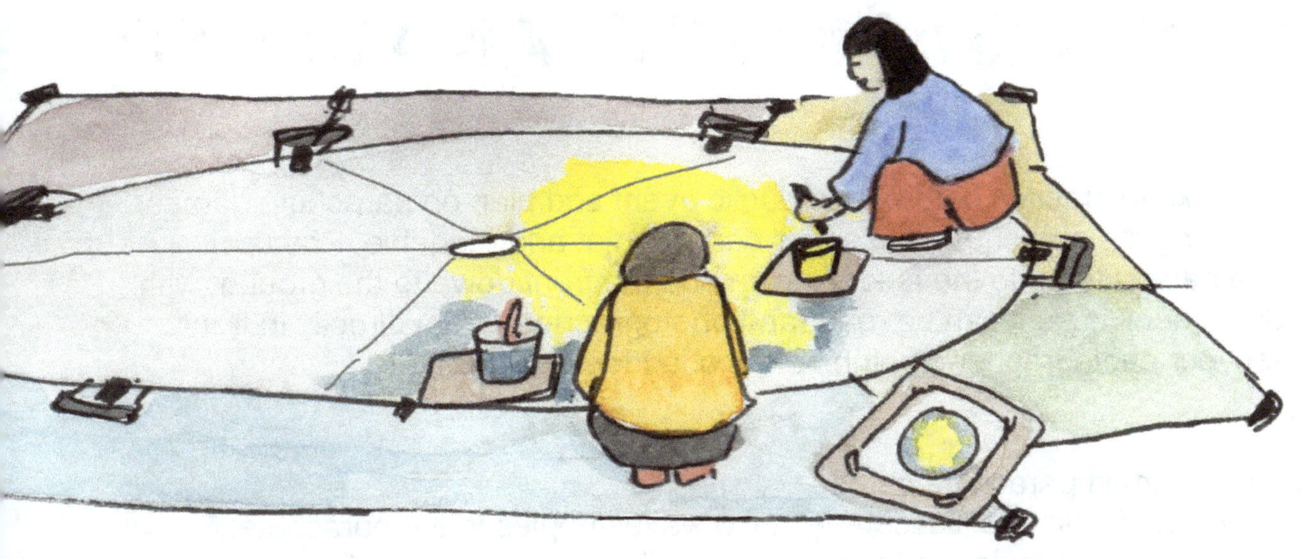

STEP SIX: PAINT

- Use bright strong colors of latex house paint or acrylic paint.
- If paint is thick thin it with about 1 part water to 3 parts paint, so it flows easily, but still covers solidly.
- Pour paint into yogurt-style containers and paint with both foam and bristle brushes of various sizes. You can set paint containers on a piece of cardboard or box top rather than directly on the parachute in case they drip.
- Start from the center and work your way out.
- If there are drips, wipe them off right away with a wet rag.
- Make sure to paint out any heavily painted areas where paint has pooled, so it will dry faster.
- Once you finish painting let the paint dry completely–for as long as you can. For the first week try not to compress tightly or fold so paint is touching paint–roll it loosely and don't compress until it's a week old. The fresh paint can still be a little tacky and stick to itself.

STEP SEVEN: MOVE IT AND USE IT!

Get some folks to practice before your public event and plan on parachute games. Practice pulling the parachute taut so it's perfectly flat and readable. Practice tipping the back side up to the holder's chin and the front down to the ground, with the holders kneeling so it can be read (and photographed!) from directly in front. Try to get your photographer up high . . . on a ladder, wall, roof, etc.

Add climate themed parachute games:
- "Make waves for climate justice!" — make waves/ripples in the parachute.
- "Rise up with the (people, earth, movement, climate justice, etc.)!" — everyone lifts up. Have everyone count off 1-2, 1-2, etc. — and while keeping the parachute up call out: "2's trade places!" . . . then all the #2 people run under the parachute, and take each other's places. You can have a short dance party in the middle.
- "Down with (Big Oil, fossil fuels, fracking, oil trains, oil/gas pipeline, etc.)" Bring parachute edges to ground.
- Throw an inflatable earth ball (like a beach ball—make or buy online) and play Save the Earth!

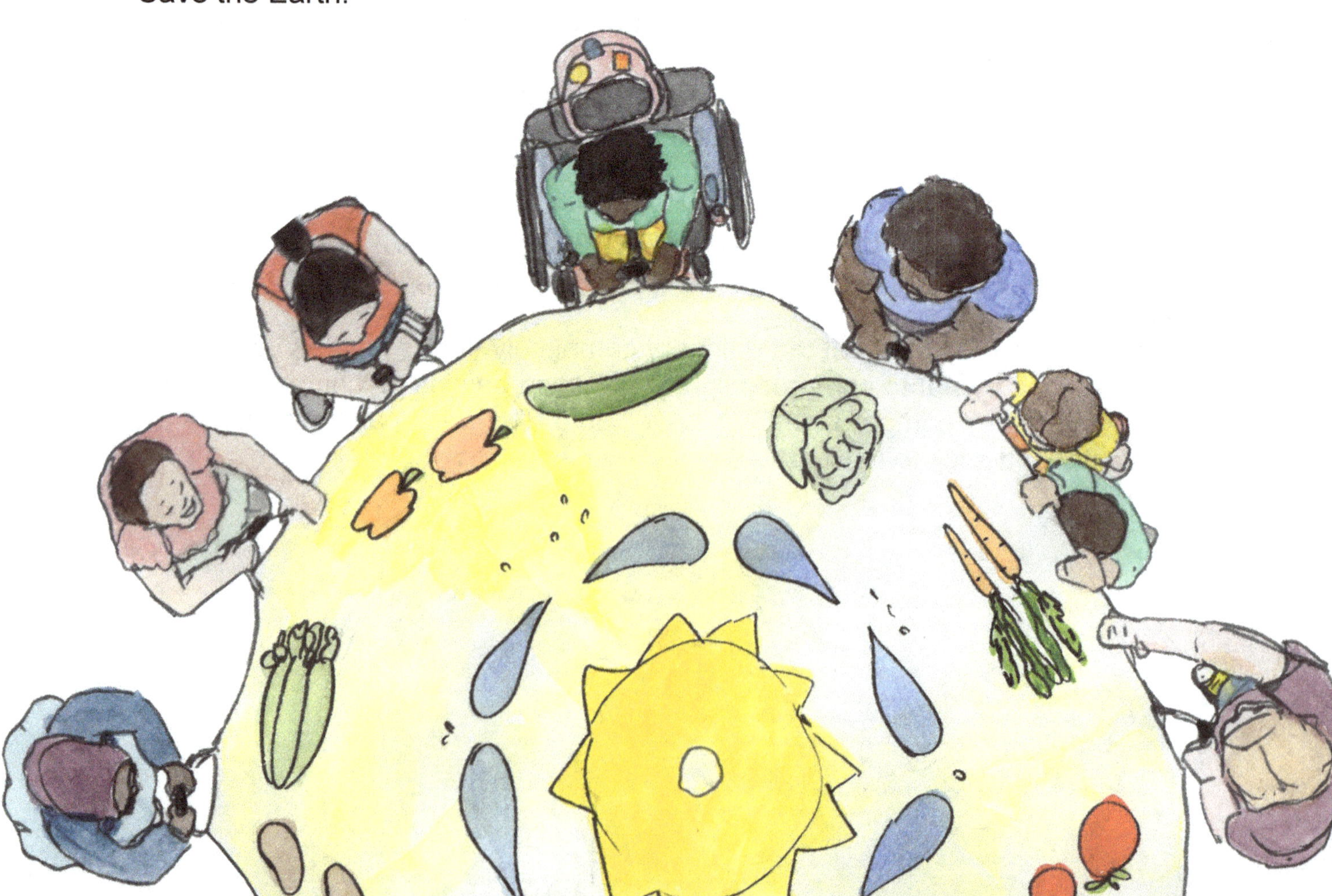

HOW TO MAKE INSTRUMENTS

Music, sound and rhythm are powerful additions to events and to the movement as a whole. Here are few simple musical instruments that can be made using easy-to-find materials. Use these to add a bit of rhythm to any march, parade, performance or bike ride.

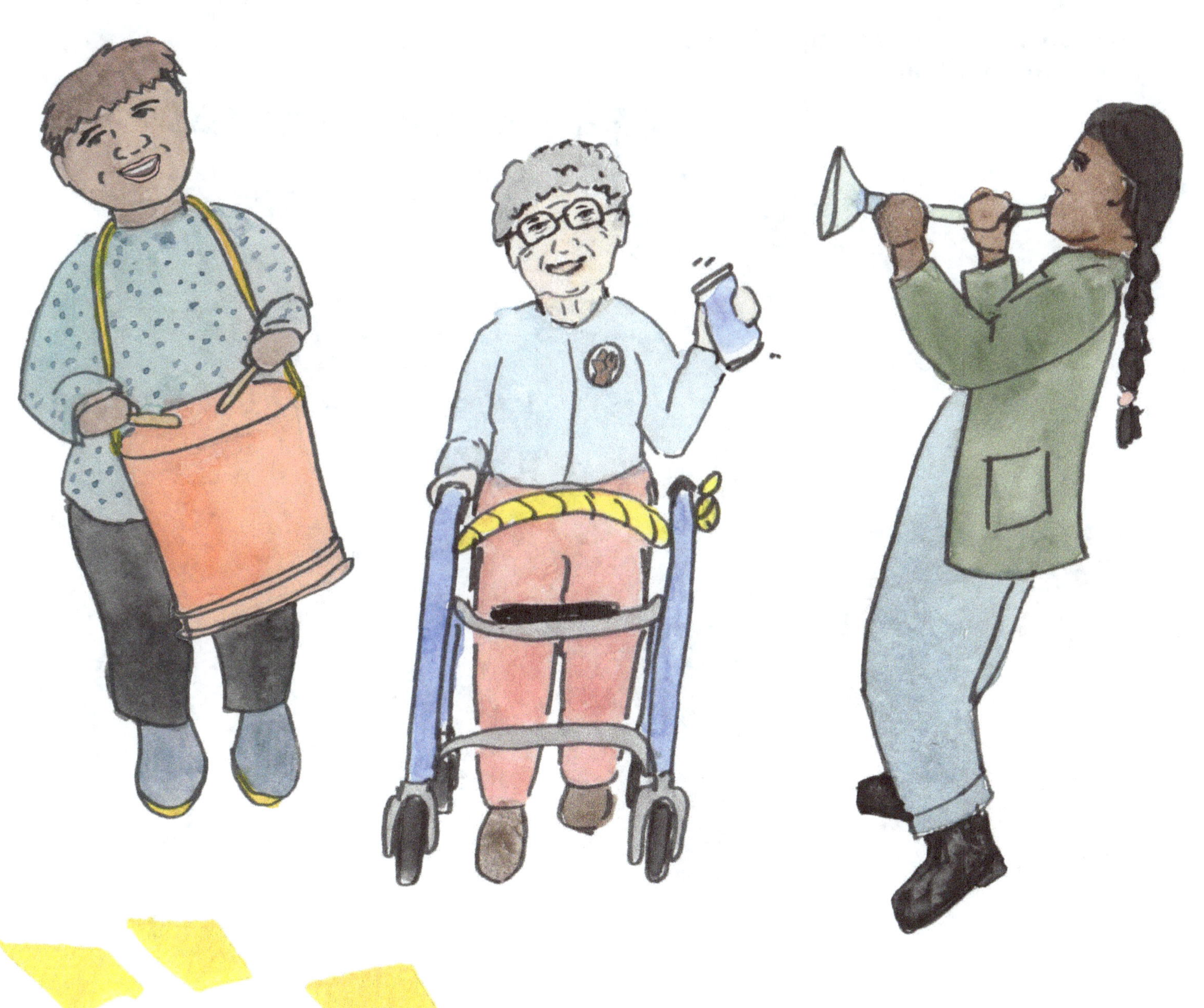

SUPPLIES

- **Buckets, cans, pots**
- **Sticks**
- **Strips of fabric**
- **Rubber tubes** - such as old hoses
- **Soda/pop cans, soda/pop bottles**
- **Rice, pebbles or beans**
- **Duct tape**
- **String**
- **Flat wood pieces**
- **Drill**
- **Utility knife or strong scissors**
- **Cardboard pieces**

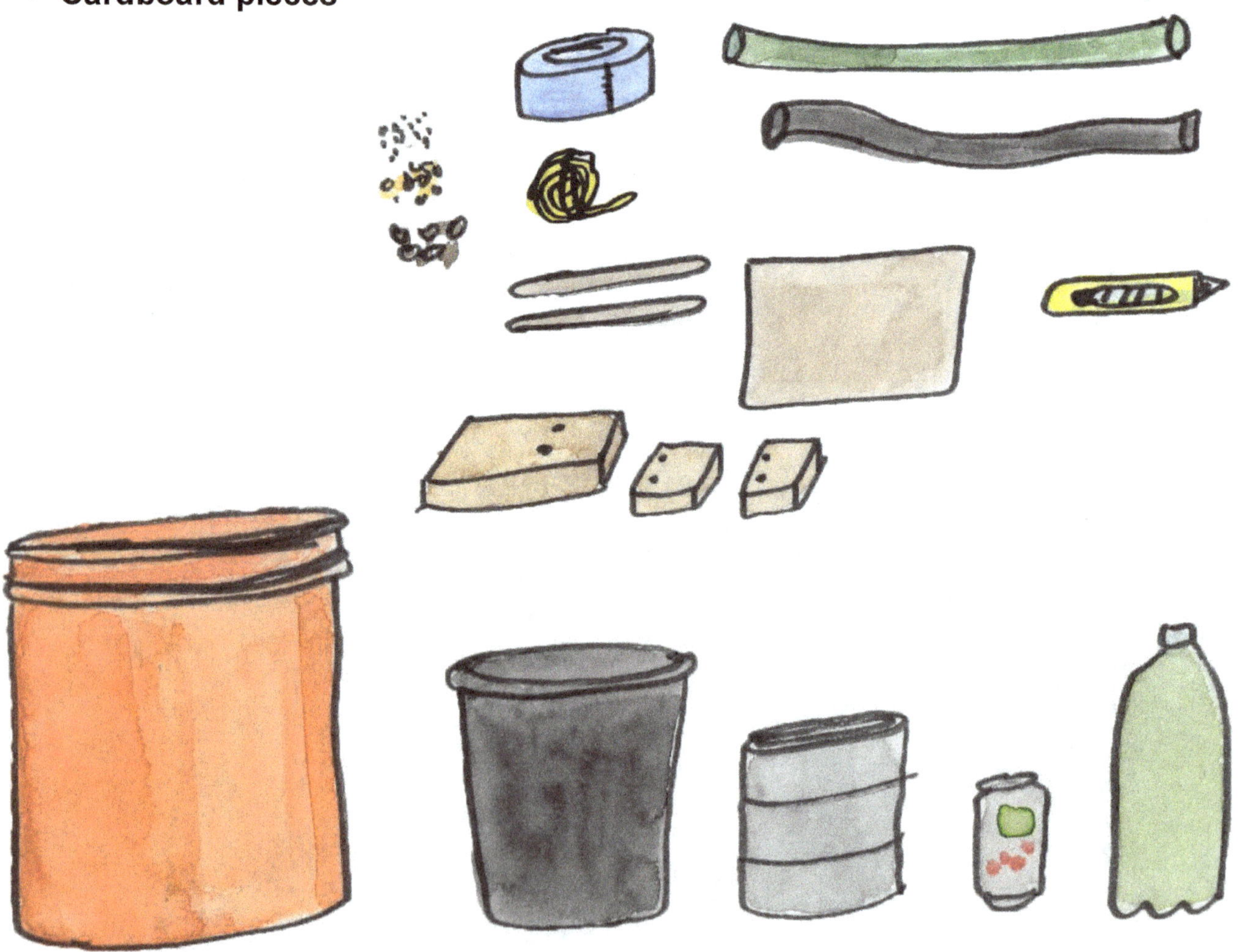

SHAKERS/MARACAS

- These little guys are super easy to make and to play. Just cut two plastic soda bottles in half and put some pebbles, rice or beans inside. Stick the two halves together, tape them up and now shake.

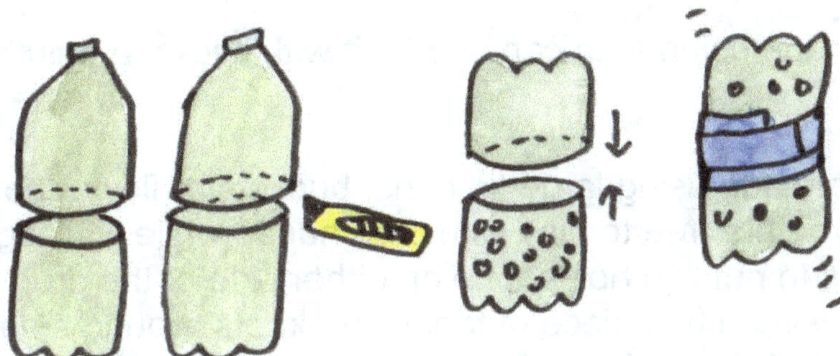

- These can also be made out of soda/pop cans. Put pebbles, beans or rice into a dry can and tape a round piece of cardboard the size of the top of the can over the top to cover the hole. Shake.

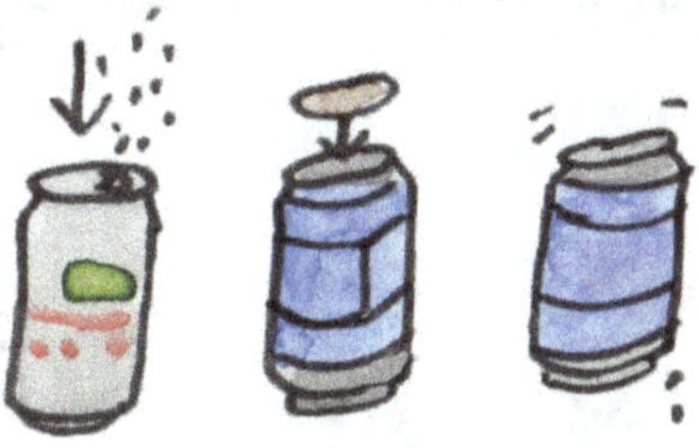

- Make lots - they sound great together. Use different materials in the cans or bottles. They will make different sounds.

- You can also paint them or cover them with fun patterned duct tape! You don't want to accidentally advertise a heartless multinational corporation.

DRUMS

Drums are perhaps the best (and simplest) of all DIY musical instruments. Drums in large numbers can have a BIG impact on the feel of an event (never underestimate the power of rhythm). Read more on organizing a drum corps below.

Small drums can be made using a tin can and hit it with sticks, a paintbrush, a large nail or a coin.

Medium drums can be made using large tin cans, buckets or flower pots. If you put a neck-strap on it' you are free to play with both hands while walking. The easiest way to do this is to put two holes, one on either side of the drum (near the top) and make a strap using a thin piece of fabric. Tie knots around small sticks inside the drums to stop the fabric from slipping out. If you don't want to make holes in good buckets, wrap rubber ties around the bucket and tie the strap to that. Hit with stick.

Big drums are the same as medium drums but bigger and louder! Use barrels, garbage bins, etc. For these you will want a different type of drumstick for deeper sounds. Tape a ball of fabric firmly around a sturdy stick (socks work well). It should look like a chicken drumstick. Next: Hit. Boom! Boom! Boom!

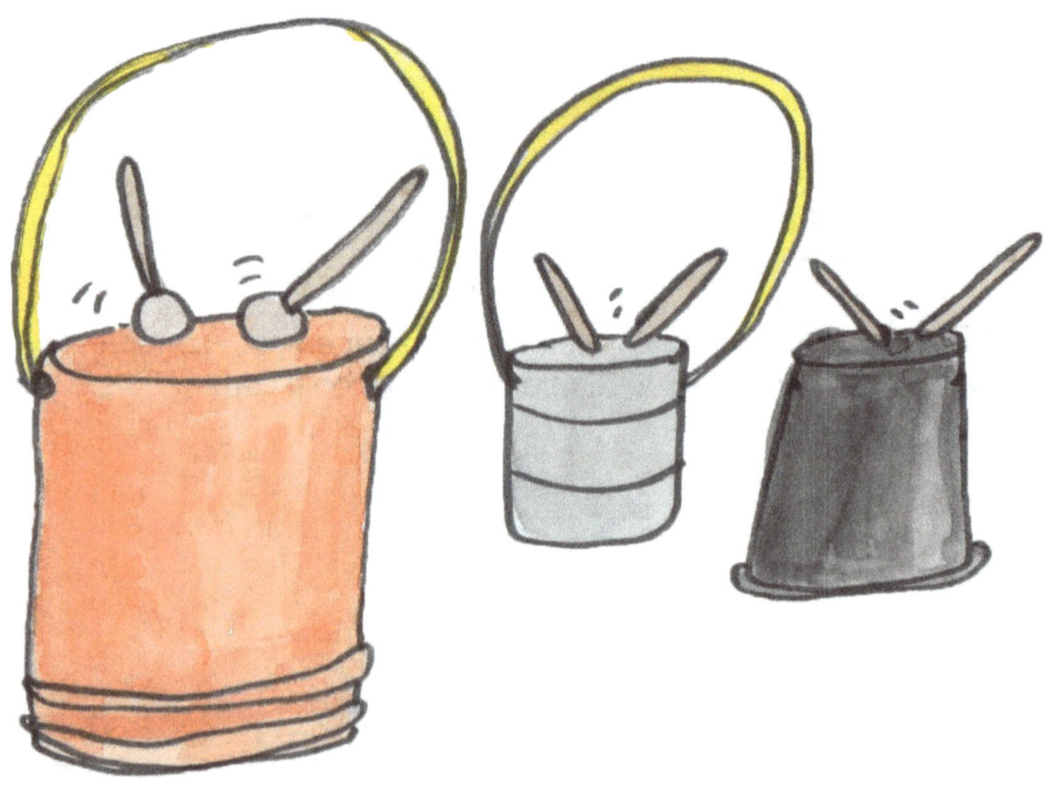

CLACKERS

Clackers are loud. All you need to make one is three pieces of flat wood (the longest piece ~5 inches/12 cm long), a drill and a piece of string.

Drill two holes through each piece of wood (you want these holes to lines up) then run the string through all three pieces and through both holes. Tie it loosely enough so the tops of the side pieces can flop around - that's what makes them clack.

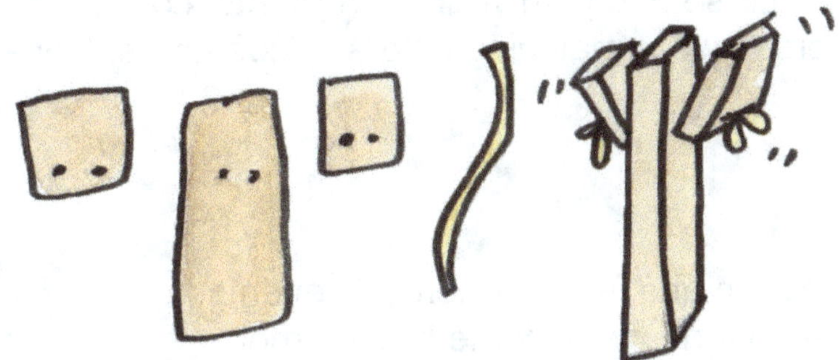

TUBE HORNS

Tube horns are ridiculous! Ridiculously fun!
Just get a short piece of hose-pipe or plastic tube (rigid or flexible) and tape the top of a soda bottle (or a cone of cardboard or a funnel) onto one end of it. Play it like a bugle. It should sound like a goose.

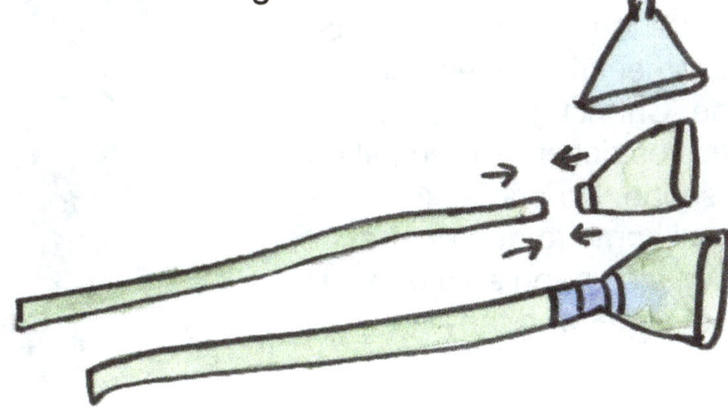

Shopping cart drum set
Put a bunch of drums, horns, whatever on a shopping cart and you can be a one person band or have a whole drum set that can move. Very useful for marches.

Now make an orchestra!

DRUM CORPS

If you want more than DIY instruments you can also intentionally invite or create a drum corps! Here are few notes on drumming!

Drumming at demonstrations and events can be as simple as getting a couple of your DIY drummers to find a song with a nice beat and practice the different parts before the event. If you have more time and energy, you can organize a bigger group to drum, rehearse and plan your instruments, coordinate with organizers and get drummers to wear matching colors or costumes. Here are a few tips.

Why drums?
They can bring rhythm and festive energy to events. Marches and demonstrations become livelier, more aggressive, more confrontational, and more fun. Drums say "No Business As Usual!" and "Let's Dance!" in a universal language. Drumming groups are easily organized compared with melodic marching bands. Sonic disruption can raise the stakes of demonstrations, legally and non-violently. Drums can win our enemies over to our side by showing them that this modern world has not dehumanized us. Drums are the quintessential tool for disrupting bureaucratic meetings when you can't, or don't want to, go inside. Chanting only gets so loud, and there are tighter restrictions on amplified sound than unamplified sound. No one asks why people bring signs, and bullhorns to demonstrations, but drums historically have also been a valuable tool in the struggle for social change, and they are resurging.

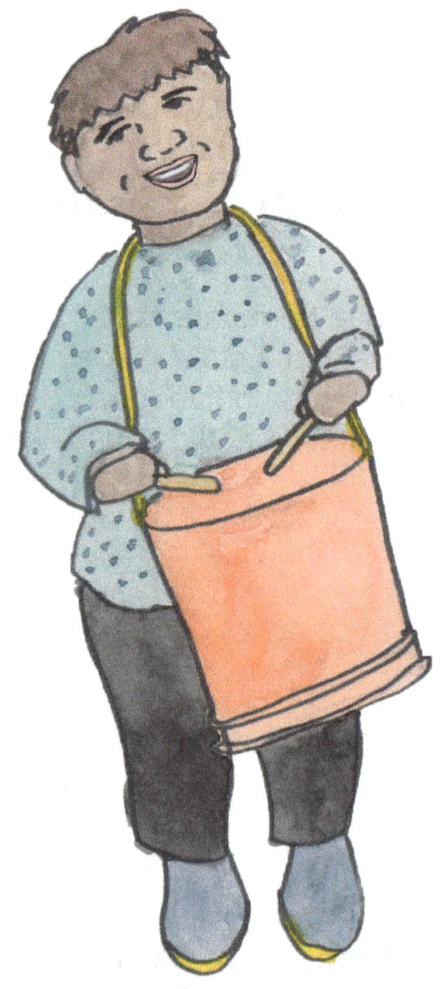

This section on Drum Corps is an excerpt from a longer manual put together by the **Super Sonic Samba School**. For more info and resources, rhythms, how to make drums and instruments and more go to: **puppetista.org/drums/**

Drum etiquette

Unfortunately, drums can also disrupt your own organization. If people aren't listening to each other, the music will be bad, and people won't be energized. Some crowds don't like drums, period, even if they're really hot. Also, drumming for demonstrations often means maximizing the volume in order to disrupt an event or reach a large crowd, but for the people right next to the drums, the noise can cause physical pain and permanent hearing damage.

Know when not to play

The social dynamics at demonstrations are different than open invitation drum circles. Drums may be used as part of a cultural ceremony or ritual — in which case it may not be appropriate for anyone to join. That would be different at an action where the sole goal is loud noise for disruption. Pay attention to the surroundings.

Playing along with chants

The message of drums is often ambiguous, so leave space for people who want to use words to clarify the issue. If you can organize it beforehand, find someone with a good sense of rhythm to lead chants that match your rhythm. Or have that person start a chant when you stop drumming. Make sure the chant leaders understand that they have to stay near the drums, and can't run ahead or fall behind. Once you're solidly locked-up with the chanters, try playing in the spaces where they are not chanting: "The people [ba-boom] united [ba-boom] will never be defeated [ba boom]."

Playing at other times

Drums are most powerful when they are played sparingly and with discipline. It's annoying to hear drums during moments of silence, candlelight vigils, when people are speaking, or even when people are clapping (it's like saying, my expressions are more important than yours, because my sound is louder). Drummers who aren't constantly evaluating their surroundings and the effect their drumming has on people, risk being totally obnoxious. It's a good habit to put your sticks away until you're ready to play as a group. Some call this the "No noodling!" rule. Another way to put it is: "Don't play unless everyone else is also playing!".

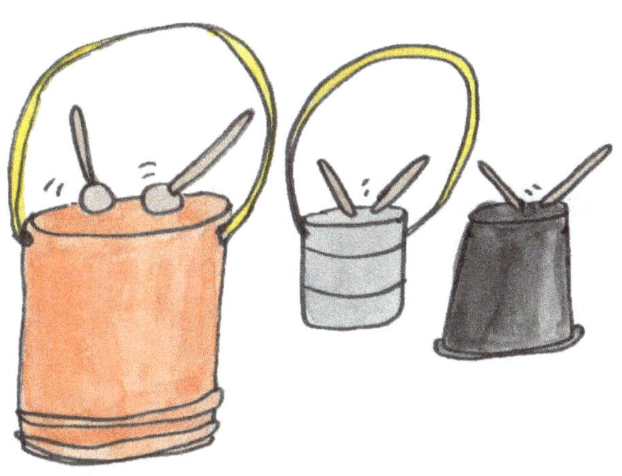

While Marching
Keep the drum section together. Don't let drummers spread out. Playing in unison
requires being able to hear the other members of your group, which becomes
more difficult the farther away you get.

Where to find drums?
Drums are everywhere: buckets, barrels, 5-gallon water bottles, pots and pans.
Avoid bringing drum sticks that look like clubs to a demonstration.

Where to find drummers?
Drummers are everywhere too, and if you bring extra drums to a demonstration
you can recruit people at the last minute to play along. Ideally, you can get a core
group of people to practice before the demonstration, where they can learn the
rhythms together,and learn the rules outlined above. Be sure to explain the rules
to everyone taking an instrument who has not practiced with the group in advance.

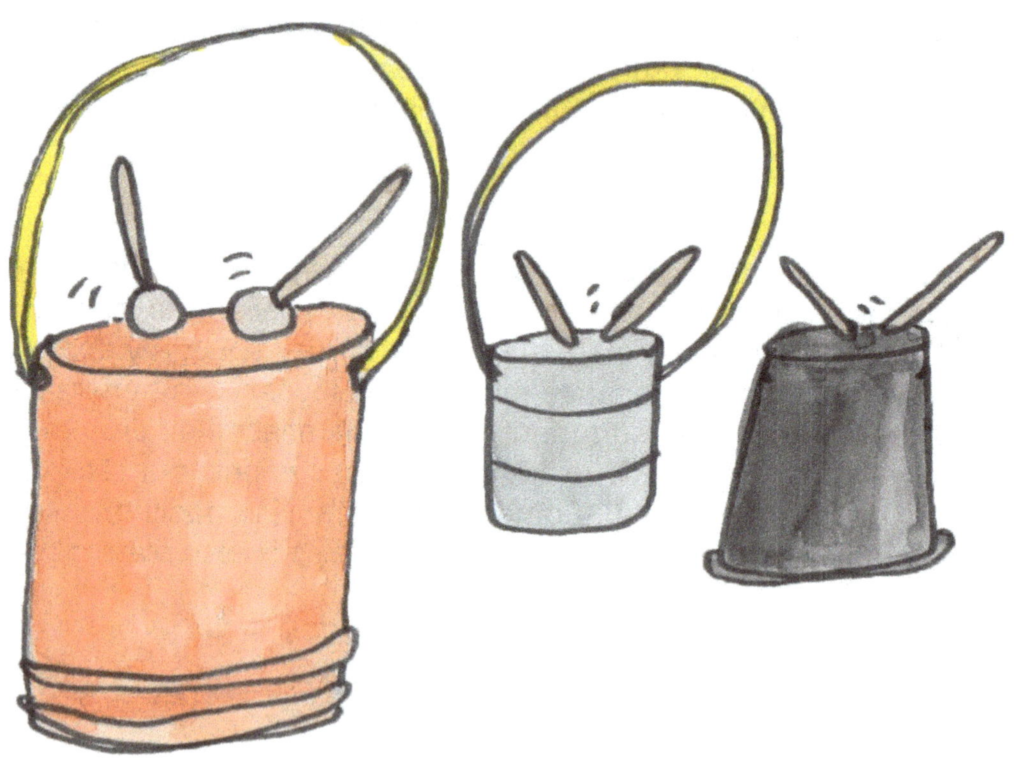

HOW TO MAKE A FLAT PUPPET

A flat puppet is often made as a sculptural representation of a specific person that is often large or life size. These instructions are for how to make a flat puppet likeness out of cardboard that can be mounted on a stick and used as a puppet.

These flat puppet likenesses (and puppets more broadly) are an effective way to draw attention to an issue that relates to a specific person or group of people (e.g., politicians). They can also be used with street theater.

There are many different ways to make puppets, especially large puppets, but the instructions here are for flat cardboard puppets, because they are simple and a fairly quick way to make puppets.

In this how-to we suggest having a photograph of the head, or the head and torso if you can. This is because it is visually compelling and makes it easy to recognize the person.

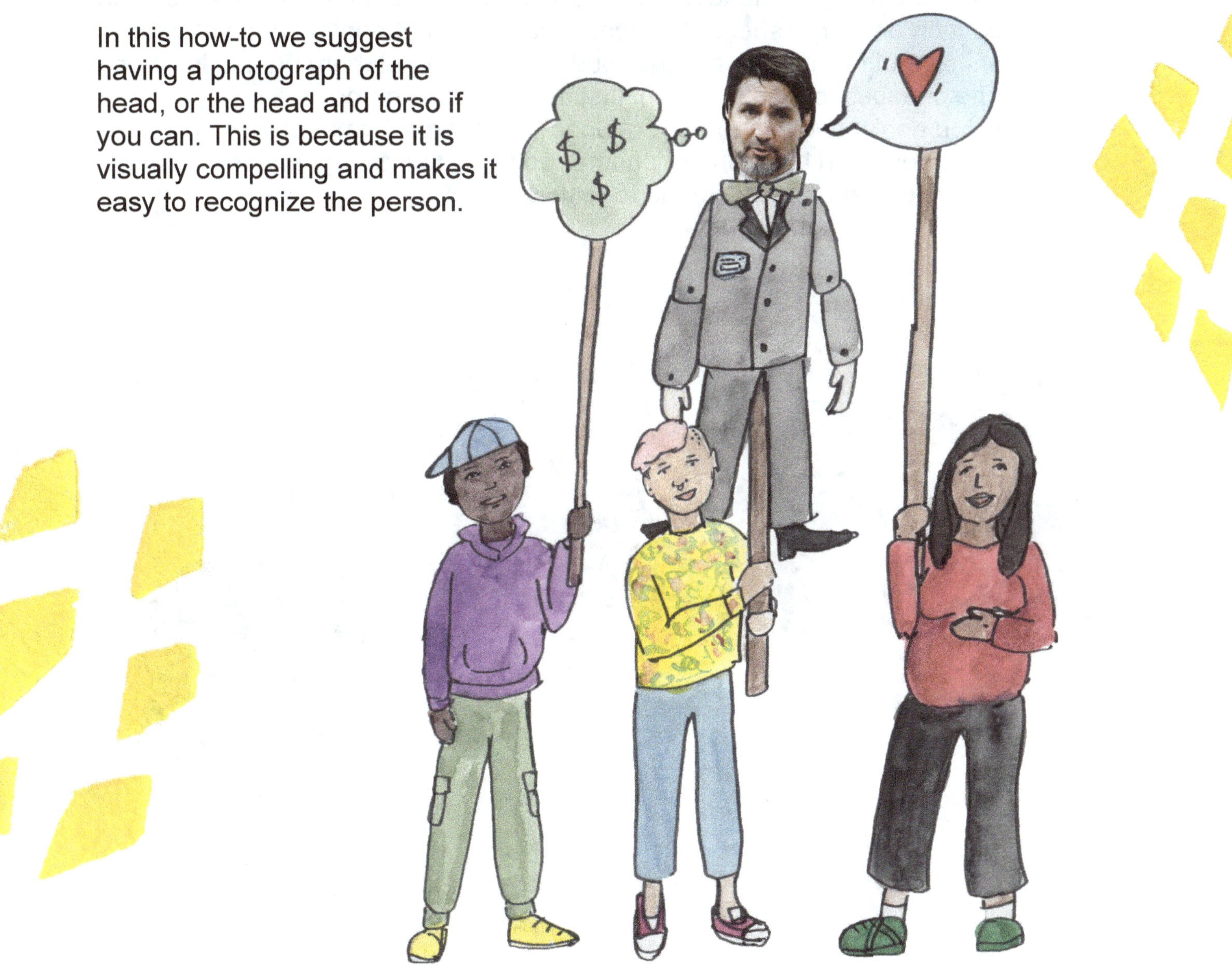

STEP ONE: GATHER SUPPLIES

- **Large pieces of cardboard**
  - Try to get appliance or furniture boxes

- **Lifesize high-resolution print-out of the person (or people)** that you want to make a flat puppet of.
  - Find a high resolution image online or scan a printed photograph at least 300 dpi. You don't want the image to look pixelated when you print it out.
  - You can decide whether to print in color or black and white.
  - You can print out **just the head of the person** and paint the rest of their body **or** you can **print an image that includes their head and torso** and use that as the puppet.
  - If you want to print head and torso, a large format printer would be best to do it on one large sheet. You can get large format printing done at print shops and if you have a bigger budget you can get them printed in color.
  - The cheapest option is to print just the face(s) at home.
  - If you don't have access to, or budget for, a large format printer to print a large head and body photo, another option is to print the image at home in sections and tile the image together.

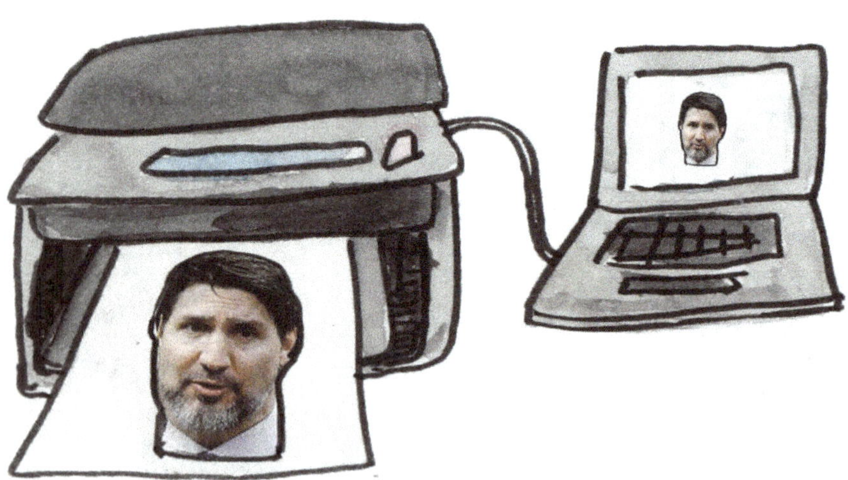

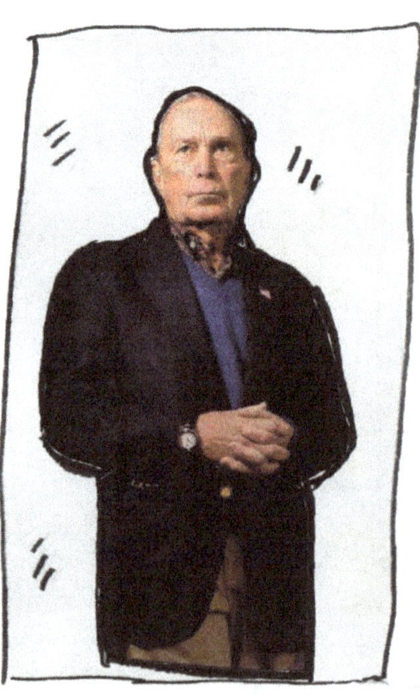

- **Acrylic or latex paint**
  Get bright strong colors of latex house paint or large (½-1 gallon) containers of acrylic. If paint is thick, thin it with about 1 part water to 3 parts paint, so it flows easily, but still covers solidly. You can pour paint into quart- sized yogurt style containers and use foam/bristle brushes of various sizes. Set paint containers on a piece of cardboard so if you drip, wipe off right away with a wet rag. Make sure to paint out any heavily painted areas where paint has pooled, so it will dry faster.
- **Paintbrushes** (have a variety of sizes, and make sure they are in good shape – not frayed)
- **Utility knife and extra blades**
- **Cutting mat** (or surface for using utility knife)
- **Scissors**
- **Yogurt containers for water and paint** (and some lids)
- **White glue or wheat paste mixture**
- **Drop cloth**
- **Pencil**
- **Masking tape** (the wider rolls are better, good quality to be sure the tape sticks)
- **Ruler(s)**
- **Sticks/poles** (8 feet /2.5 m - can be cut in half or to other lengths)
- **Latex varnish or clear acrylic medium** (optional - to paint a clear coat for increased weather durability)
- **Rubber ties** (can be cut from old bicycle inner tubes)

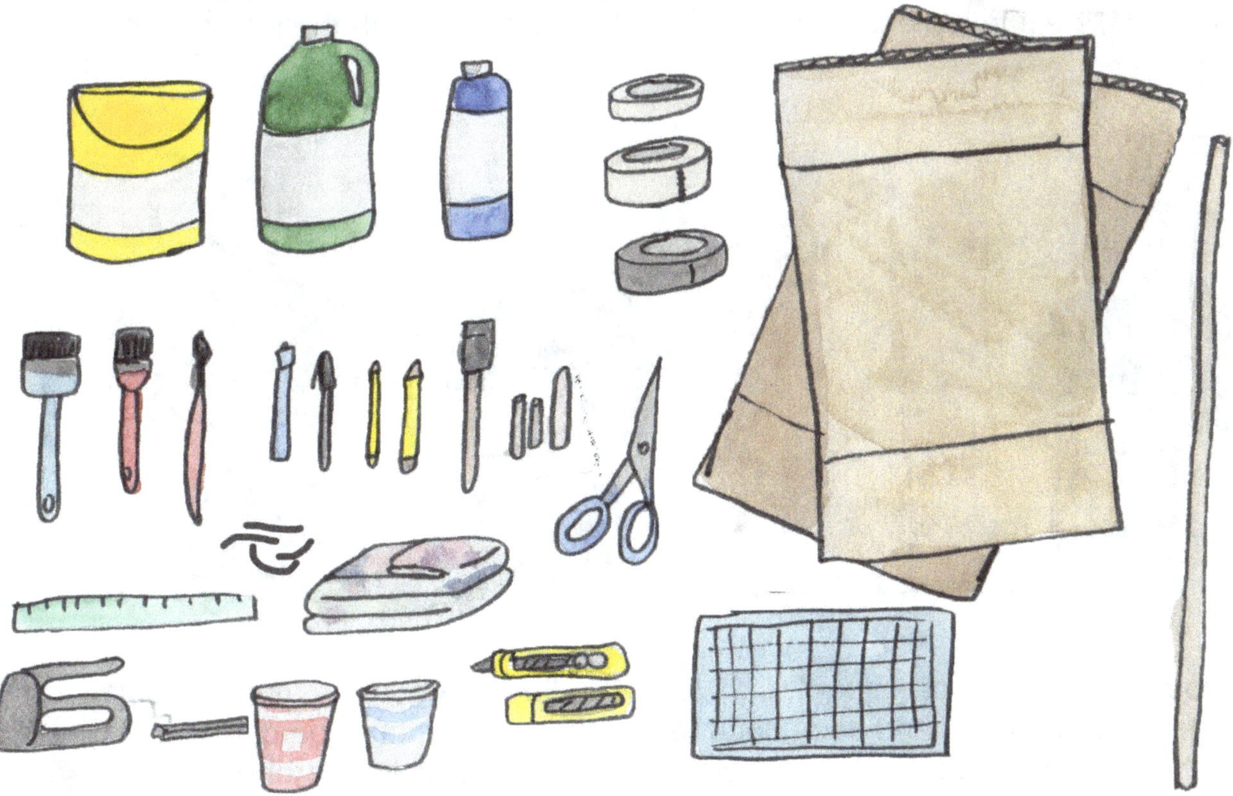

STEP TWO: PASTE, DRAW AND CUT

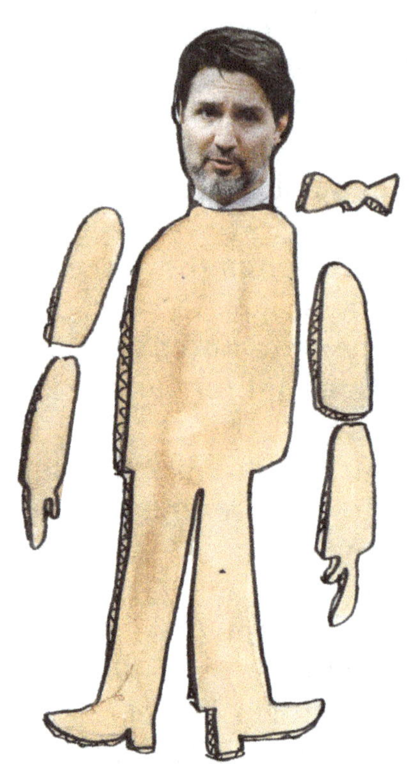

Photo head and painted body
- Cut out the head photo and white glue or wheat-paste it to the top of your cardboard.
- Draw the neck and torso/body attached to the head. You can exaggerate the outfit or features of the outfit for effect.
- Draw the arms in sections separately. You can draw the legs on the same piece of cardboard as the head and torso if the cardboard is big enough, or draw them separately and attach in step five.
- Once you have all your shapes drawn, cut everything out of the cardboard.

Photo head and torso
- If you are using a printed head and torso, cut the image out and glue or wheat-paste it to a piece of cardboard. Then cut it out with the utility knife.

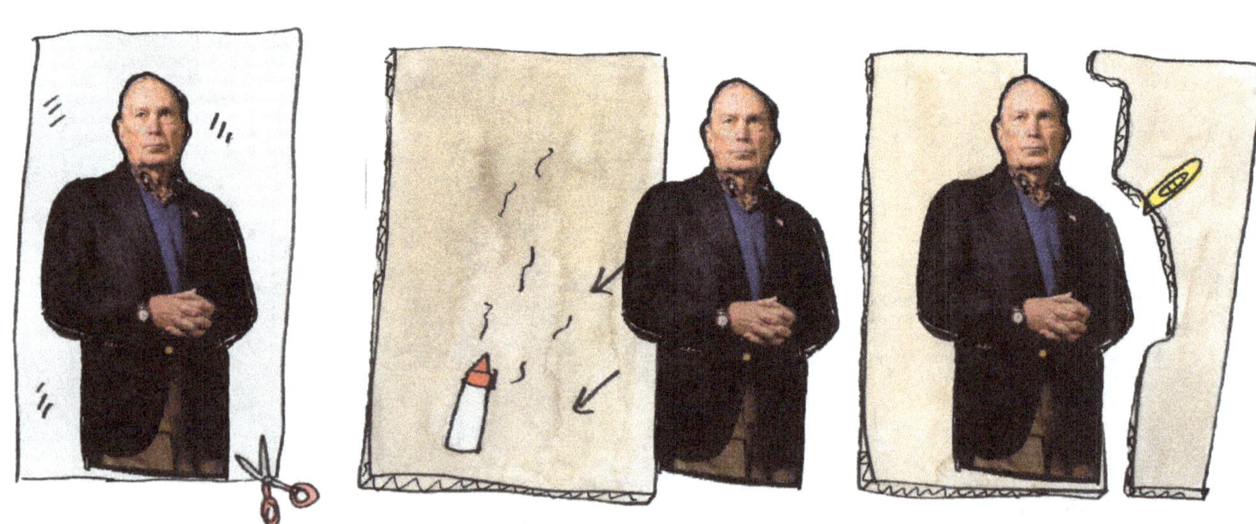

* If you have enough cardboard and want your flat puppet to be more durable, cut the shape of the head and body out of a second layer of cardboard, and then the two sheets of cardboard can be taped together, similar to the cardboard sign instructions.

STEP THREE: PAINT

Photo head and painted body
- Paint in your drawing of the body, arms and legs using acrylic or latex paint.

Photo head and torso
- If you printed out the whole head and torso, you can paint with a clear coat for increased weather resistance (something such as your wheatpaste mixture if it's clear, a varnish or clear acrylic medium). This is optional.

If you printed your image in black and white you can paint a wash on top of the photo to add some color. A wash is a watered down paint, so you aren't covering up the whole photograph with thick paint. If you do a wash don't make it so watery that it wrecks the image. Test out your wash out on some cardboard and photo scraps before you paint on the flat puppet.

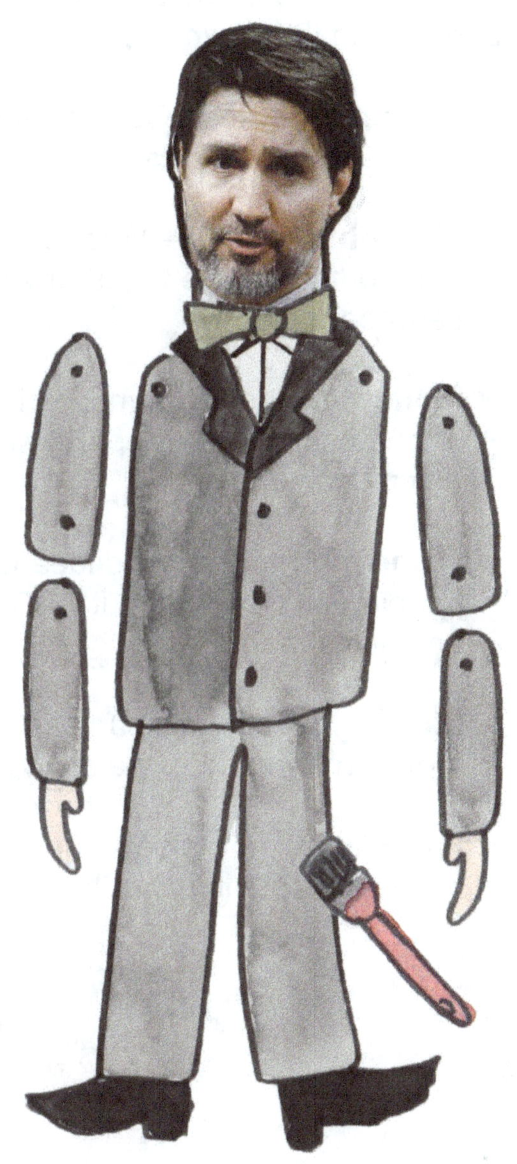

Let the paint dry completely – for as long as you can. For the first week try not to compress tightly or fold so paint is touching paint. The fresh paint can still be a little tacky and stick to itself.

STEP FOUR: ACCESSORIES

Use accessories to help share your message. You can create accessories with leftover cardboard or find other props to attach to the flat puppet. Props can also be attached to their own stick to be held beside the flat puppet.

- **Speech bubbles** - Can be used to draw attention to something someone has said. Use real quotes. Quotes can be on cardboard signs on their own sticks.

- **Thought bubbles** – What are they really thinking? You can connect the different parts of the bubble together with wire or thin sticks taped to the back of the cardboard pieces.

- **Money** - You can put money into politicians hands. These can either be painted or photocopied. If you put a wire hook on the hand these can be removable. Velcro works too.

- **Name tags** - It's a good idea to put the person's name directly on them, in case people don't know who it is. This also makes sure their name gets into photos and newspapers.

- **Signs** - Flat puppets can carry their own signs. Attach them to both hands and they can swing (e.g., salary $10,000,000).

- **Fat cats** - Flat puppets can have friends. Who do they spend time with? These can just be painted cardboard on a stick.

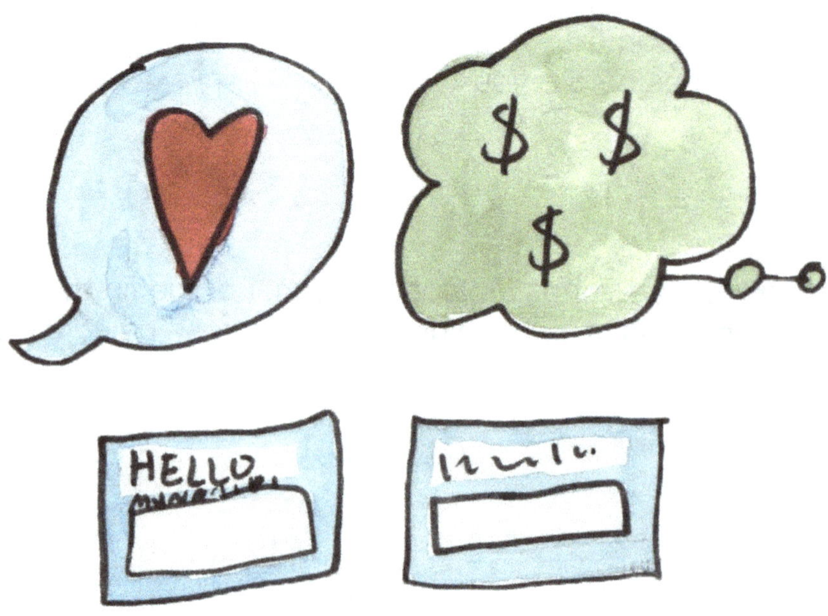

STEP FIVE: ASSEMBLE

Have all your parts ready:
- Painted body and photo head, (and possibly legs) made from a single piece of cardboard.
- Arms (and possibly legs) as separate cardboard sections.

Attach the arms to the body using rubber ties (bicycle inner tubes cut into strips). Have small holes at the joints where you want pieces to attach and run the tie through the overlapping holes. Tie big knots on each side of the rubber ties so they don't slip through. This allows the arms to swing and be moved.

Mount on pole
- Attach your pole to the back using staples with glue (waterproof if it may get rained on) or by making small holes through the cardboard on either side of the pole and running a rubber tie through the holes and around the pole and tying in a knot. Do this in three places on the flat puppet. To make the cardboard stronger, you can add extra pieces of cardboard between the pole and flat puppet (rubber ties should pass through these too). This can stop the cardboard from ripping out.

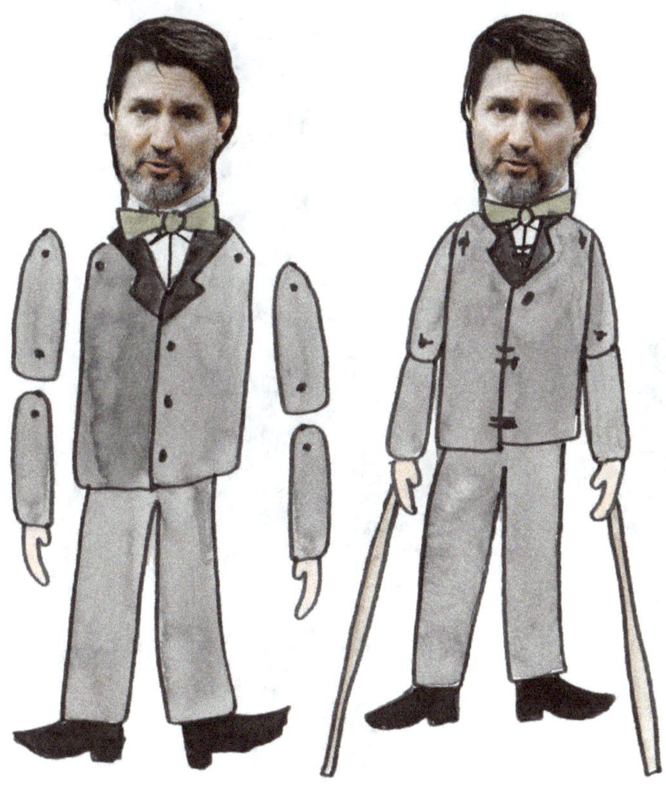

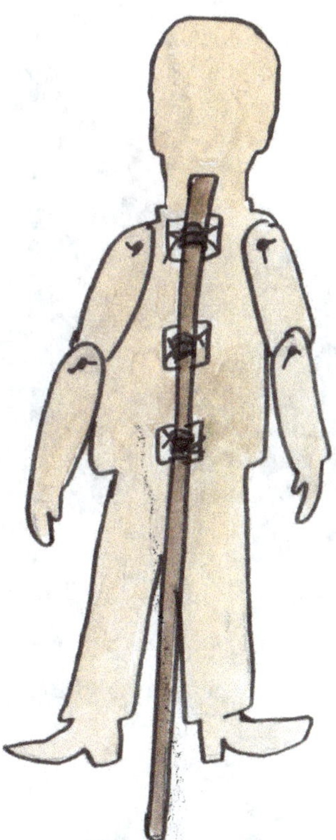

- Hand poles optional. This allows arms to be raised.
- If using rubber ties to attach, put them in areas of the clothing where they blend in.

STEP SIX: TAKE TO THE STREETS

It's great to use the flat puppets as part of a larger plan to confront a person or bring attention to an issue, so you can strategically plan to make these to accompany a campaign or action.

Get plenty of people to volunteer ahead to carry the flat puppets. You can have people trade off during an event if they are holding them for a long time. Practice standing and then moving together. Arrange the flat puppets together in a visible space as part of your demonstration.

Place other visuals, accessories or people in front and below them. Hold the flat puppets above head level so the whole body/message is visible. You can put them up on 8 feet/2.5 m sticks to make it easy to keep them high. Be intentional and creative with your choreography. For example, they could move, slow motion, single file around the space, turned to face the people/camera/public. The people holding them are part of the visual/puppet, so it's great if those folks can be focussed and only do that and not have other tasks.

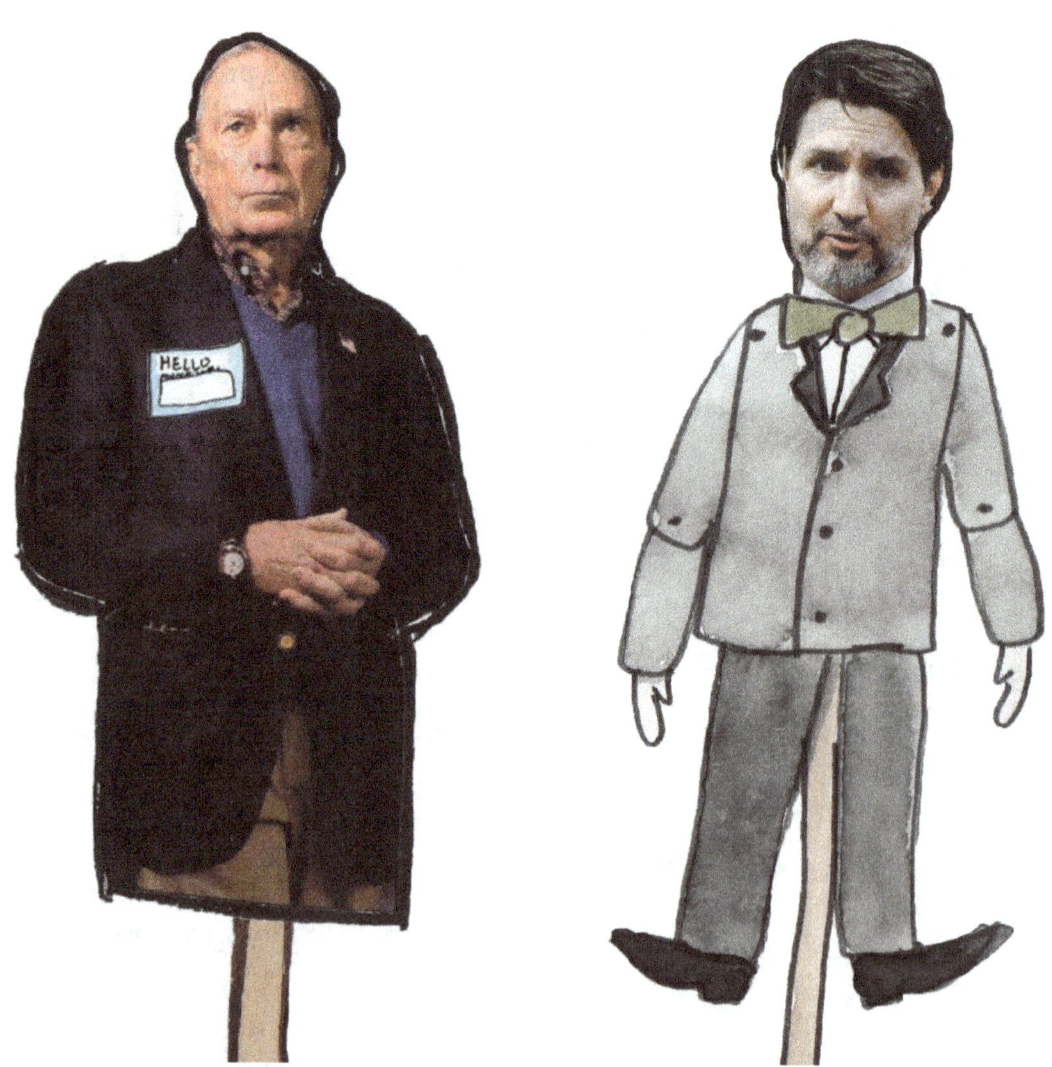

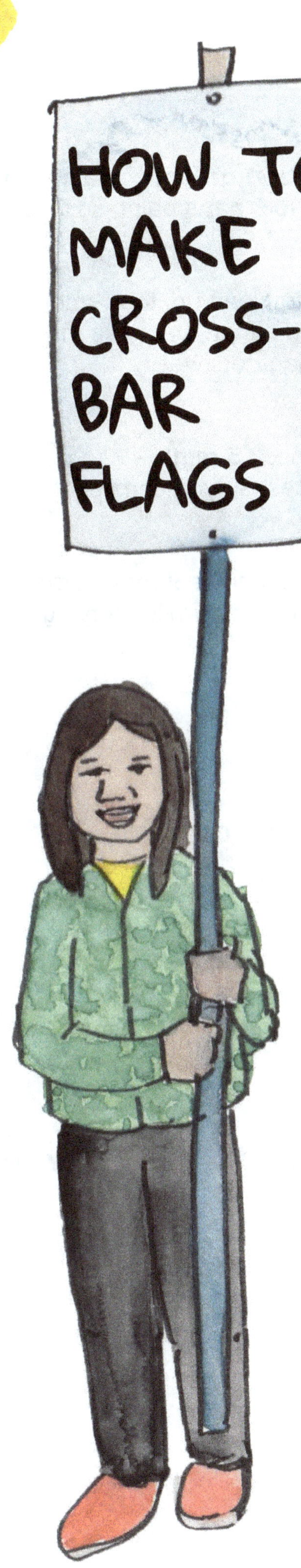

Crossbar flags are painted, stencilled or screen-printed fabric flags attached to a vertical pole. They are very visible and easy to carry. It is visually impactful to create as many crossbar flags as you can with similar designs, that can all be carried together.

Crossbar flags can be carried above people's heads, adding height to a group of people at the same time as keeping the images and messaging visible even in a crowd.

STEP ONE: GATHER SUPPLIES

- **White or light colored fabric**
  Try to find lightweight muslin, cotton, polyester or other lightweight non-stretchy white fabrics such as old sheets. You can sometimes get old sheets for free from hotels or industrial laundry companies.

- **Latex or acrylic paint**
  Get bright strong colors of latex house paint or large (½-1 gallon) containers of acrylic. If paint is thick, thin it with about 1 part water to 3 parts paint, so it flows easily, but still covers solidly.

  Don't use oil-based paints because they are difficult to clean up, they smell badly and they dry slowly. Tempera paints aren't good either, because they aren't permanent and will run and wash away if the flag gets wet.

- **Lath sticks**
  Flat narrow wood strips (about 1 1/2 x 1/3 inch/38mm x 8.5 mm).
  Lath is used to back plaster walls and for fence trellises, so you can find it garden centers or construction supplies.

- **Wood poles** (8 feet tall, 1x2 inches/2.44 meters tall, 25mm x 50mm) 'furring strips.' Make sure they don't have big knots that might break while carrying.

- **Duct tape**
- **Paper**
- **Pencil and marker**
- **Staple gun and staples**
- **Drop cloth**
- **Paint brushes** (have a variety of sizes and good quality – not frayed)
- **Old yogurt or plastic containers** (and some lids)
- **Measuring tape**
- **Scissors**
- **Straight edge** (ruler or meter stick)
- **Screws** (3/4 to 1 inch/19mm - 25mm) 'truss head' (washer head) screws or wood or sheet-metal screws.
- **Cordless drill**

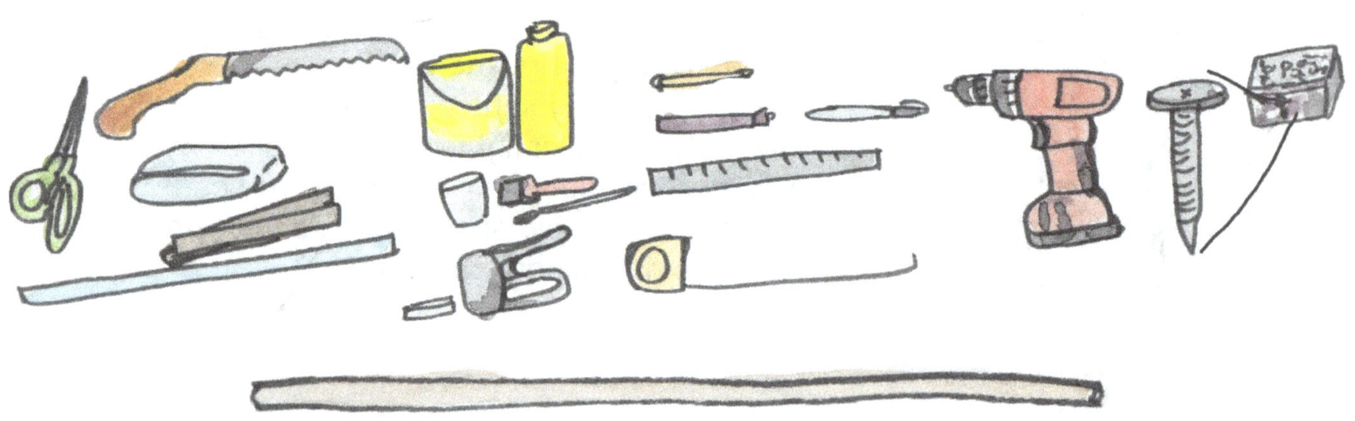

STEP TWO: CUT FABRIC

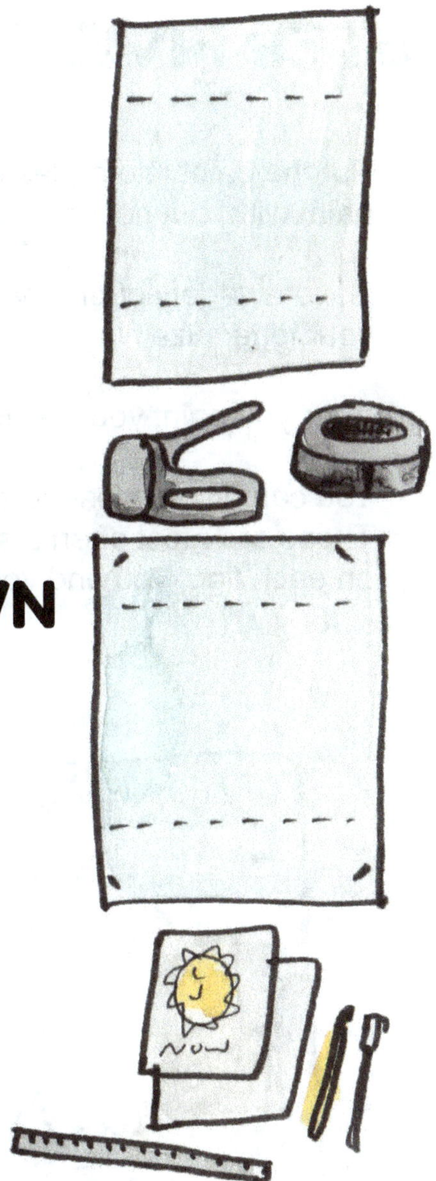

- Spread out your fabric and measure it. Measure out flags about 24 x 40 inches/60cm x 100cm. (This will include ~6 inches/15 cm of excess fabric to wrap around the top and bottom sticks.)

- Adjust the flag size to make best use of the size of fabric you have and to best fit your desired design. Cut with the grain of the fabric to get started, and then tear the fabric to size.

STEP THREE: STAPLE DOWN

- Create a painting table with a sheet of not-too-rough plywood placed on top of a table or sawhorses, and then staple the flag fabric to the plywood in four corners, pulling it tightly so there are no wrinkles. You can also do this with masking or duct tape.

- If you don't have plywood you can also lay a drop cloth down underneath your flag. Tape the drop cloth to keep it from moving and tape the flag fabric to the drop cloth.

STEP FOUR: DESIGN

Draw your design — first on paper, then on the flag fabric.

Design tips:
- Less is more; sticking with a few shorter words and simple bold images makes your message stronger and easier to read.
- A light/dark color contrast also makes it more readable. One option is to paint a light color over the whole flag as a primer, let it dry, then draw your design and paint with much darker colors.
- When you are planning and drawing your design on the fabric make sure you leave extra fabric (6 inches/15 cm) at the top and bottom to wrap around the sticks.

STEP FIVE: PAINT

- Put the paint into a plastic container and thin with water a bit to make it easier to paint with, but not so much it bleeds or looks thin.

- Have a variety of brushes, including foam brushes, to match your paintbrush to your letter size.

- After you paint your design let the flag dry, then pull it off the plywood.

- You can also choose to screen print or stencil a design on the flags instead. These are most often a single color design, so after you print the base design on each flag, you and volunteers can add a hand painted element to each flag.

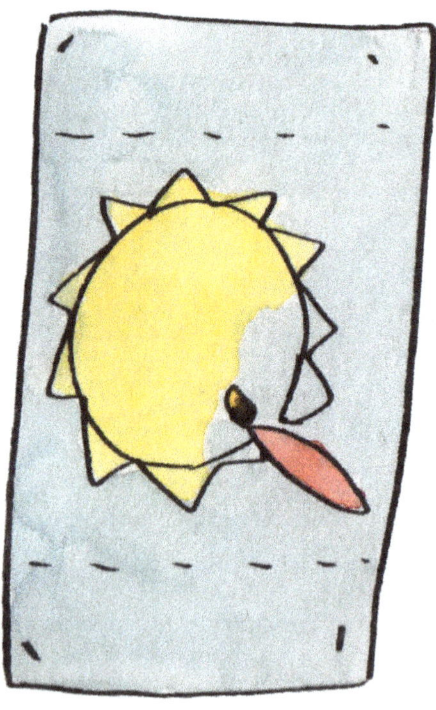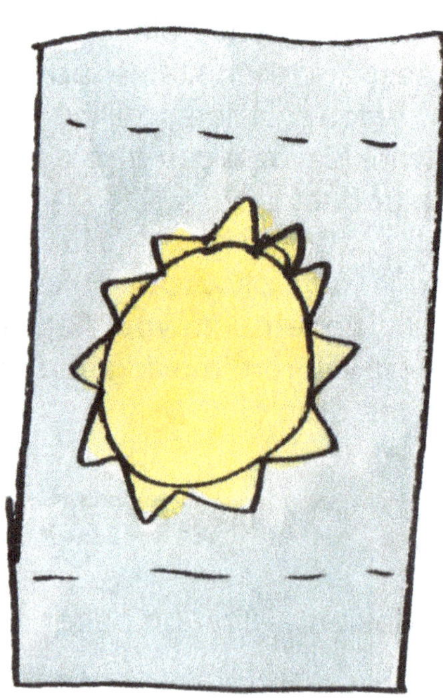

STEP SIX: ATTACH TO POLES

- Cut the lath slightly shorter than the width of the fabric, so it's not visible or sharp.

- Use a staple gun to staple the edge of the fabric to the outside edge of the stick. Roll the stick over twice and securely staple the fabric to the stick. Use ¼ inch/ 6 mm staples–or just shorter that the wood thickness, to avoid sharp edges. Repeat this step at the top and bottom of each flag.

- Then attach your vertical flag pole using the screws and the cordless drill with a phillips bit to screw the middle of the top and bottom of the flag sticks securely into the vertical flagpole. You can either assemble them onsite to make transport easier or else bundle them up 4-6 per bundle for transport and carrying to site.

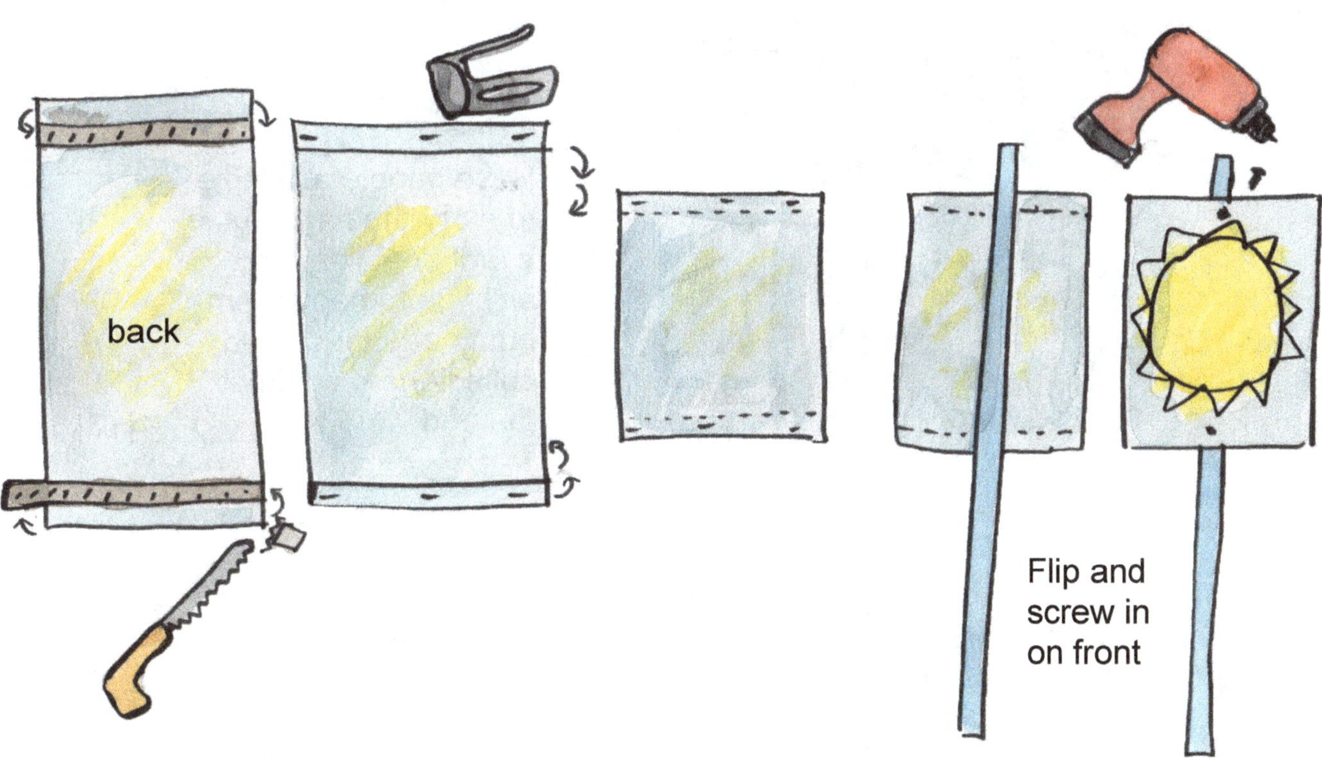

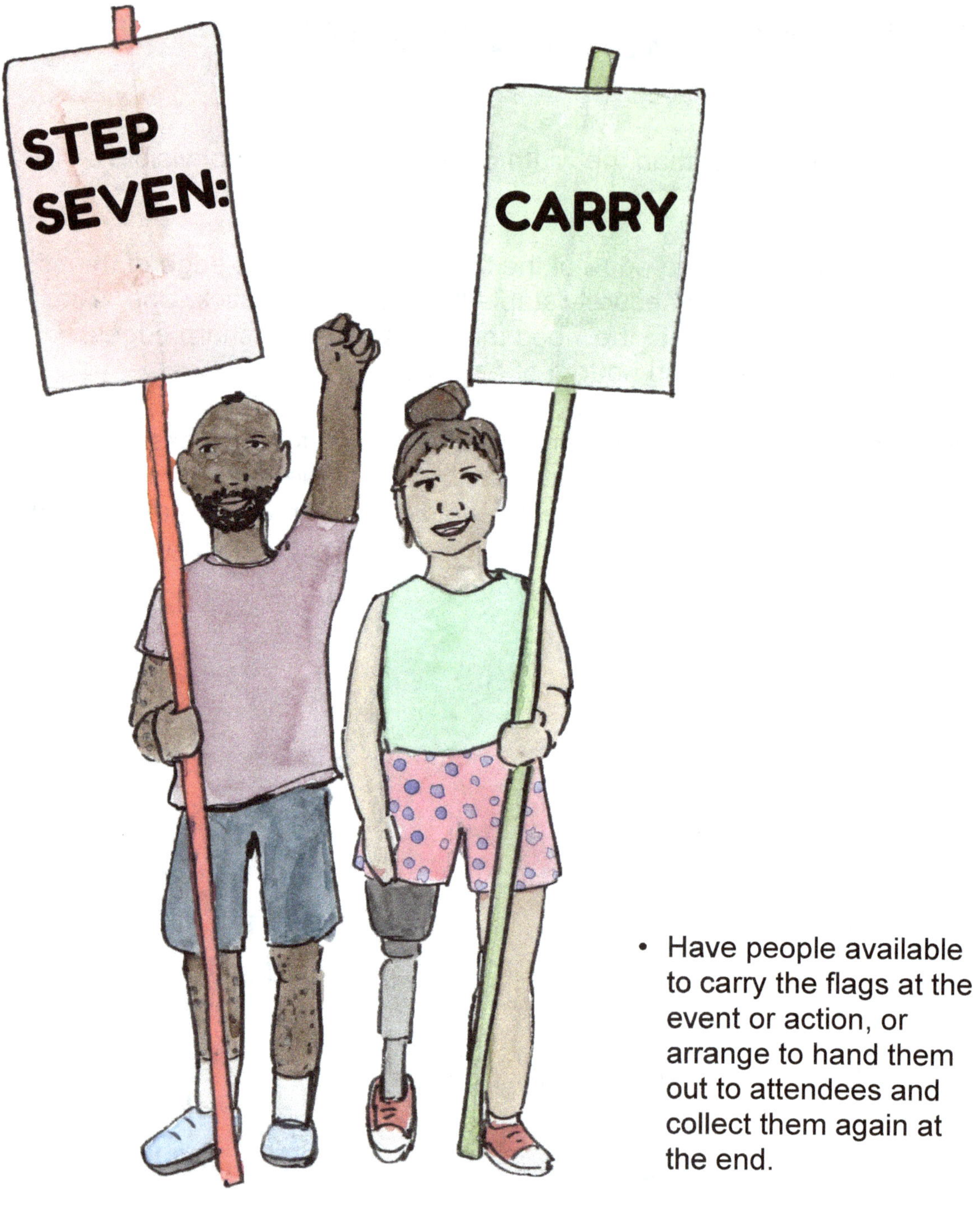

- Have people available to carry the flags at the event or action, or arrange to hand them out to attendees and collect them again at the end.

- When the flags are being carried, check if they are in the best place and facing the right direction. Consider if you want them to move as a line or groups of flags, or with some choreography.

- They can make a powerful visual, especially positioned right behind a hand-held banner people hold below their heads.

HOW TO MAKE CARDBOARD SIGNS

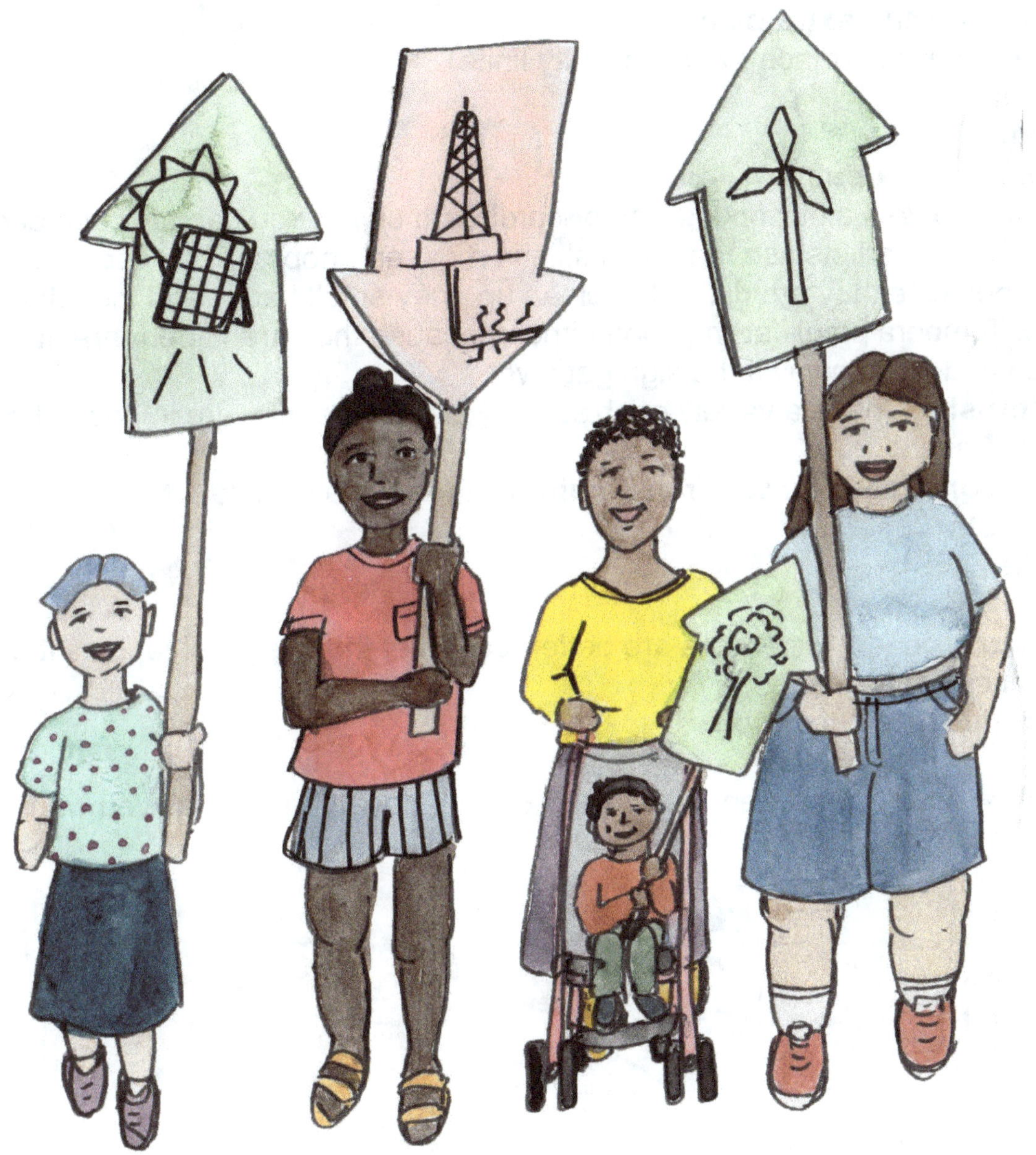

Cardboard signs are an easy and effective way to take a rectangular poster sign to the next level! You can double your impact by making the shape of the cardboard sign communicate your message in addition to any text or imagery on the sign itself. You can create a series of cardboard signs to be carried together.

STEP ONE: GATHER SUPPLIES

- **Cardboard** (Large pieces are better)
- **Utility knife and extra blades**
- **Cutting mat** (or surface for using utility knife)
- **Scissors**
- **Stapler**
- **Acrylic or latex paint**
  Old latex house paint works great for cardboard signs. You can also use acrylic paint (the kind artists use, and available in most art shops). Don't use oil-based paints because they are difficult to clean up, they smell badly, and they dry slowly. Tempera paints aren't good either, because they aren't permanent and will run and wash away if the sign gets wet.
- **Paintbrushes** (have a variety of sizes, and make sure they are in good shape, i.e., not frayed)
- **Yogurt containers for water and paint** (with lids, if available)
- **Drop cloth**
- **Pencils**
- **Paper**
- **Masking tape** (the wider rolls are better; don't get the cheapest tape as it often lacks effective adhesive)
- **Wood glue or white glue**
- **Ruler**
- **Sticks or poles** (Between 1 - 2.5 m, 3-8 feet - based on how tall you want the signs)

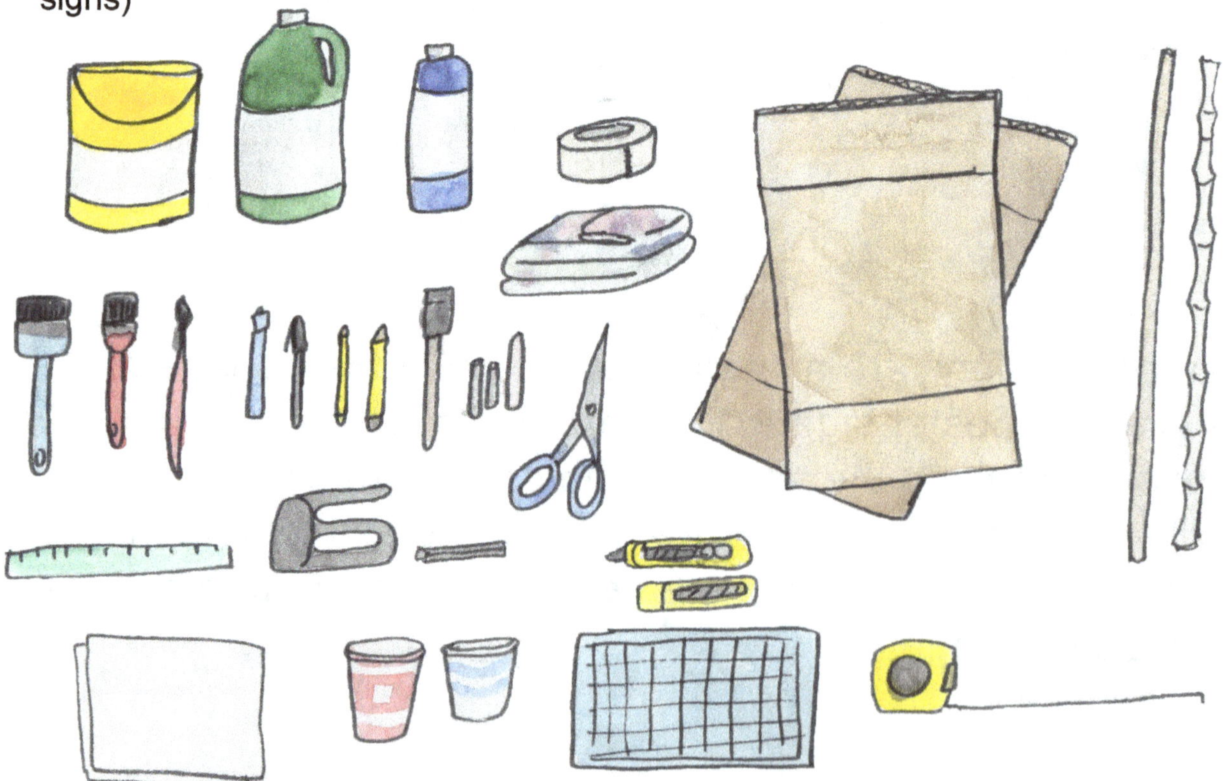

STEP TWO: DRAW AND CUT OUT SHAPES

- Design your image on scrap paper and then scale and draw it on the cardboard. Use the ruler for straight lines and even distances. For circles you can draw around a big bucket, a lid, or use a pencil tied to a string like a compass.
- Draw and cut out the first side, and then trace the shape onto another piece of cardboard for the second side. (This makes the two sides symmetrical as you'll later attach them back-to-back.) Keep any text or images printed on the cardboard on the inside of the sign and the clean side of the cardboard to the outside of the sign.
- Cut the cardboard out with a utility knife with a sharp blade with a cutting mat underneath, or some heavy duty scissors.
- If you are making many signs you can keep tracing the original.
- If you are making something like sunflowers the pole can act as the stem and you can add cardboard leaves partway down the pole.

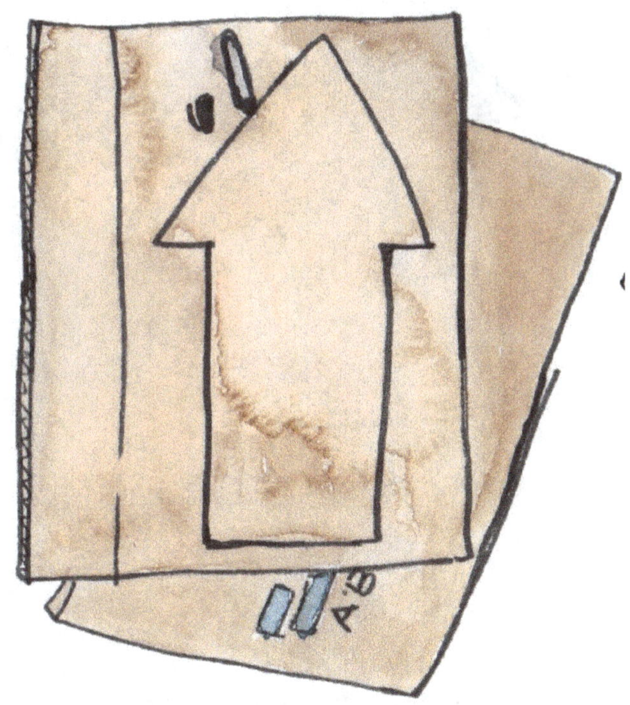

These are the steps for double sided signs, which are great because the message can be read from both the front and the back and the signs are sturdier. Cardboard signs can also be made single sided which is faster and simpler, so decide based on the amount of time you have and if you will reuse the signs often. Here is a demo in this video starting around 1:25. https://vimeo.com/161333820

STEP THREE: GLUE AND TAPE

- First glue your two pieces of cardboard together. Put white glue or wood glue near edge of the shapes and sandwich two cut-outs together. Leave about 5 cm/ 2 inches at the bottom of the shapes unglued– this will be your opening to slide in a stick. Make a pencil mark on the outside of the sign so you know where the unglued section is.
- Next use masking tape (2 inch/5cm width) to tape around the glued edges, leaving the unglued part untaped for the pole. Put half of the tape on one side, folding the other half over to the other side of the sign. Cut the masking tape with scissors instead of ripping it to help the edges look clean.

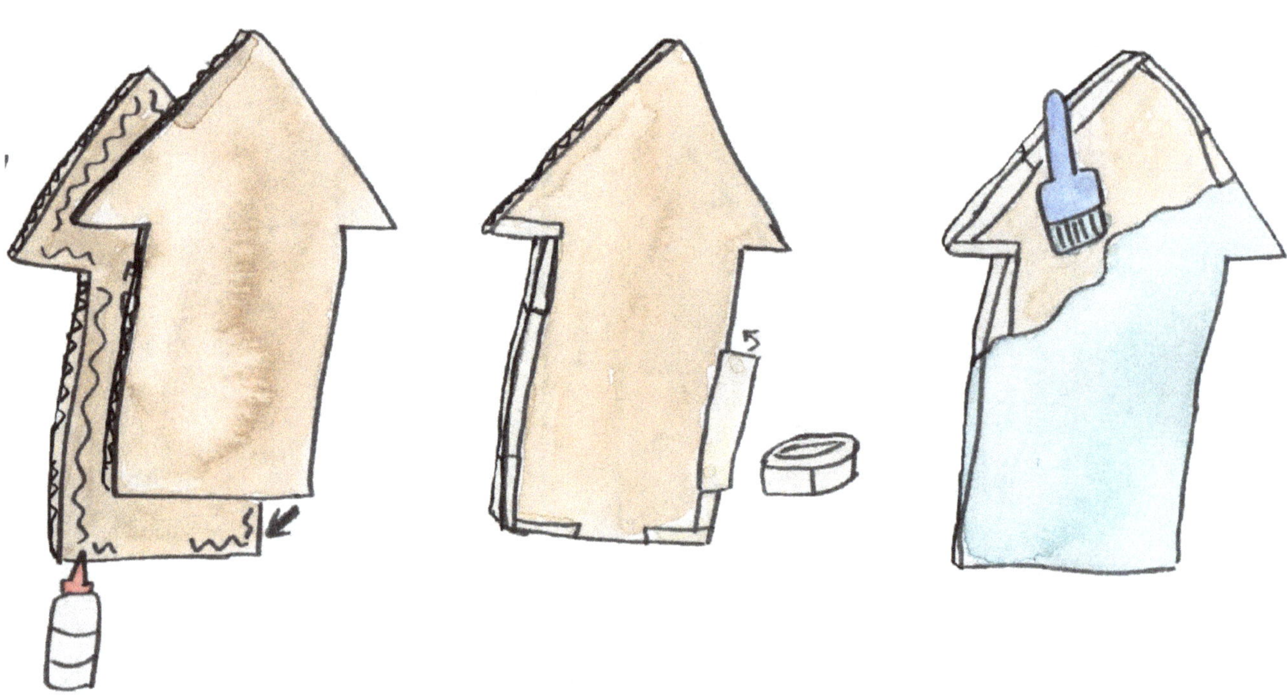

STEP FOUR: PAINT BACKGROUND

- Paint background with acrylic or latex paint. Paint both sides and the edges. Depending on the paint quality and opacity, you may need two coats of paint.
- Semigloss paint can handle rain best!
- You can also paint the poles so they are colorful too!

STEP FIVE: ADD LETTERING AND DETAILS

After the background is dry paint the text and any missing details, like messaging you're using, or detail in the object. Draw your design out on paper first. Both painting and stenciling work well on cardboard signs. Decorate both sides of the sign so it can be read in both directions.

- **Paint**
  Aim for high contrast between background and text colors to help make the text visible. Keep all slogans or phrases short and bold.

- **Stencil**
  If you are making many signs that are the same size and with the same message(s), you can make a stencil for your design. You can then spray paint or use a roller to stencil the design onto your signs.

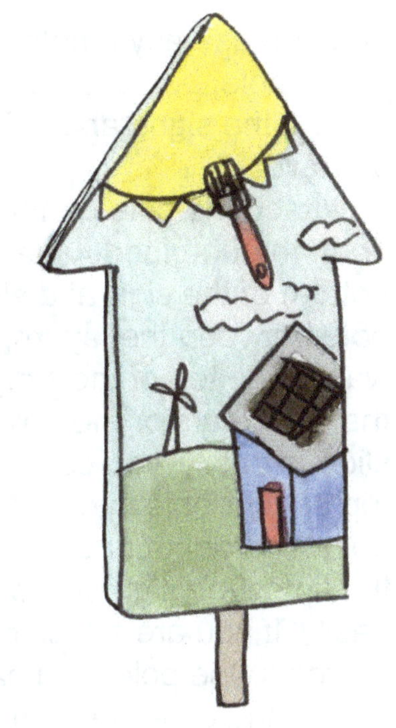

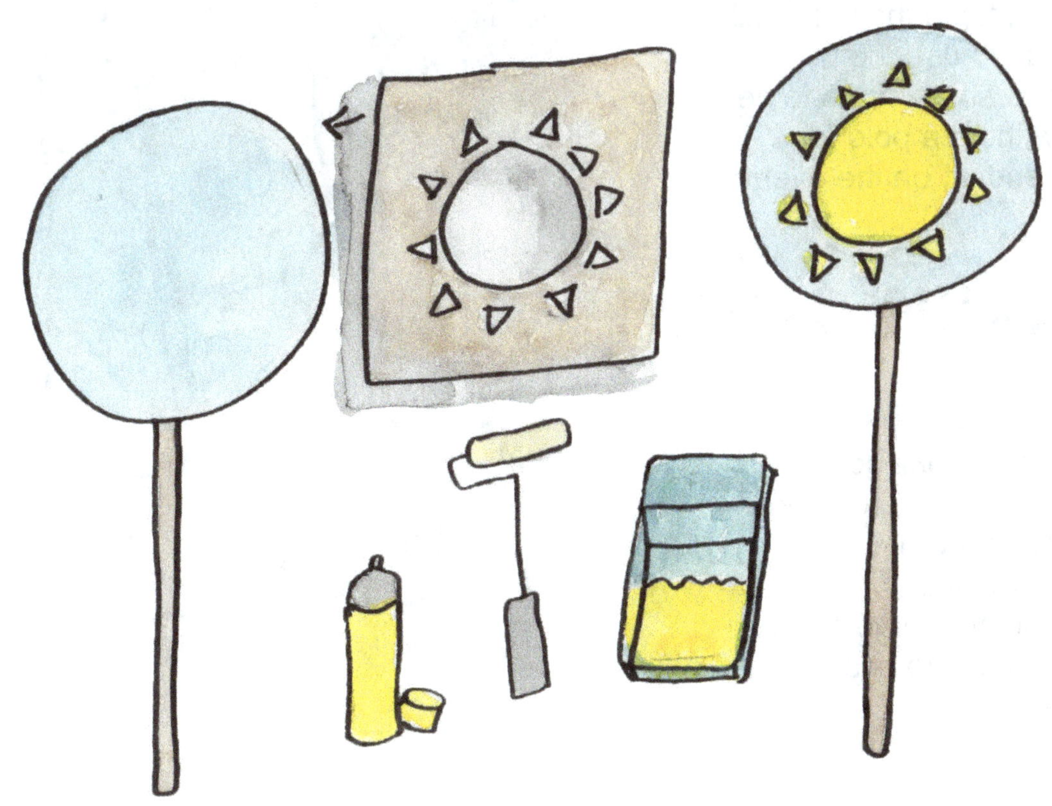

STEP SIX: ATTACH TO POLE

- You can use any length of flat or round pole, but taller is great for getting the signs above heads in a crowd.
- To attach the pole gently pry open the un-glued, untaped bottom of the sign and slide the pole between the layers, all the way to the top of the sign. If it the tape tears or the pole won't slide in easily, you can cut the top of your pole into a 45 degree point and/or put duct tape over the tip so the sign slides on easily. If you are attaching leaves to the pole, you can staple and glue them on.
- You can staple the poles in place if they feel loose at all, but if you want to be able to take the poles out easily (for transport or re-use) don't staple them in until you are ready to use them.
- You can leave some signs to be hand held without a pole for variety, depending on the event.

STEP SEVEN: CARRY!

- Have all your signs ready to go for your event. It looks good to have a group of people carrying the signs close together for a strong visual impact.
- Make sure you get some good photos of the signs to share on social media!

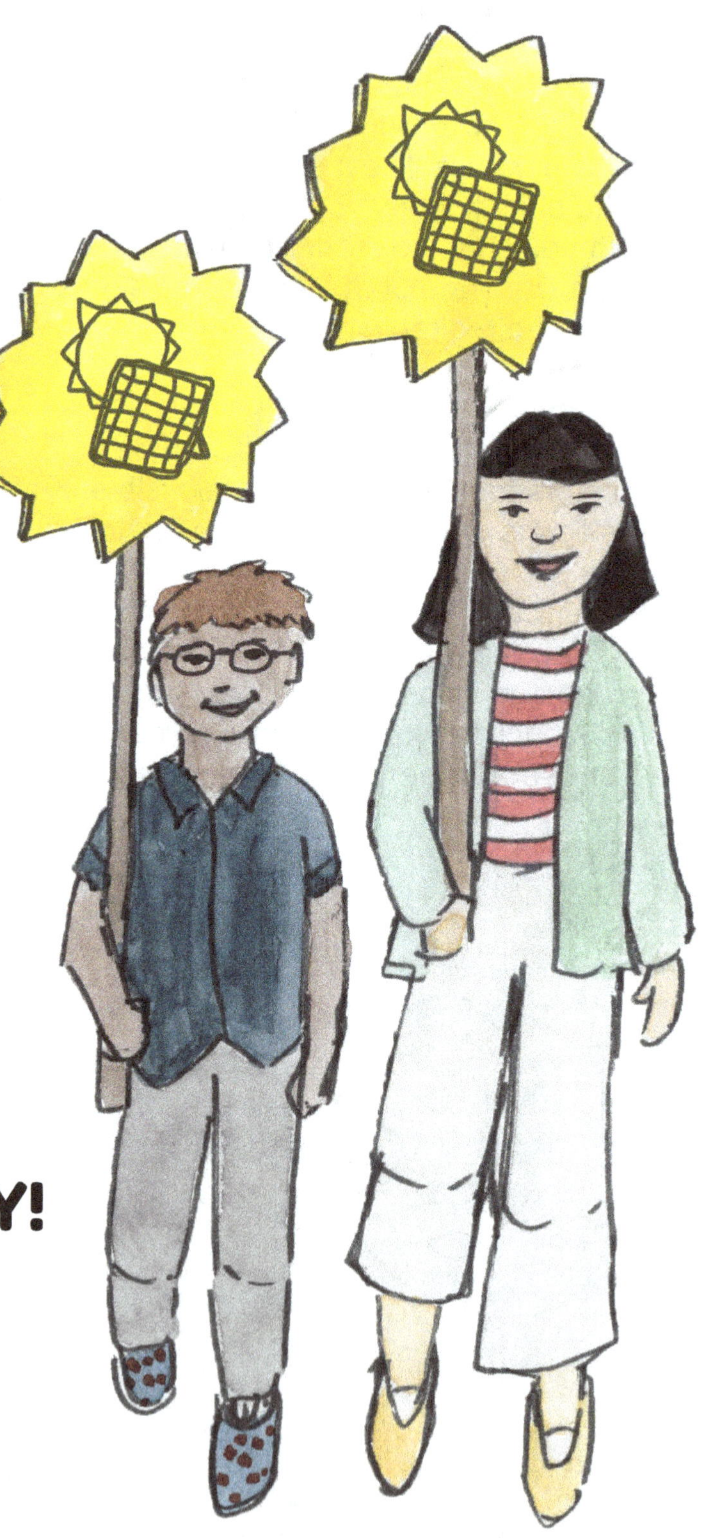

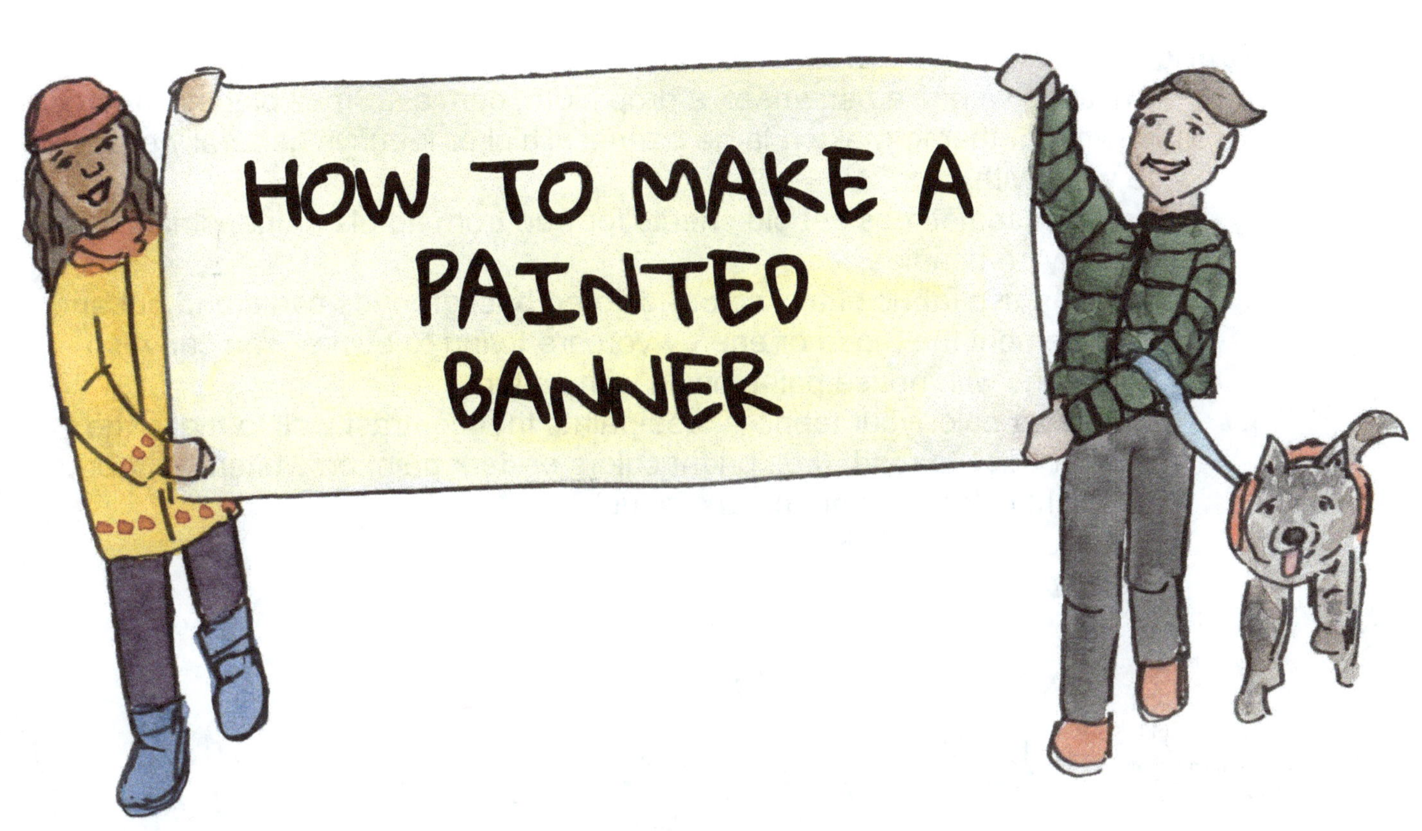

Banners are probably the most traditional way to share messages. They can easily make your message clearly visible to passersby and in photographs. Banners are versatile and can be held, hung, suspended, carried or 'dropped'. They can be used at rallies, marches, for bird dogging, as backdrops, or hung on fences or windows.

STEP ONE: GATHER SUPPLIES

- **Fabric**
    - Anything works: a bed sheet, a drop cloth, canvas. Small pieces can be sewn together to make a large banner. Thicker fabric is generally easier to work with.
    - You can sometimes get old sheets for free from hotels or industrial laundry companies.
    - You can use fabric of any color - colored backgrounds can stand out and complement the mood or energy you are trying to evoke. You can also dye fabric with house paint mixed with water.
    - Whatever color your fabric is, use paints that contrast well to make the banner easy to read. (i.e,. bright colors or dark paint on white/light fabric and light colored paint on dark fabric).

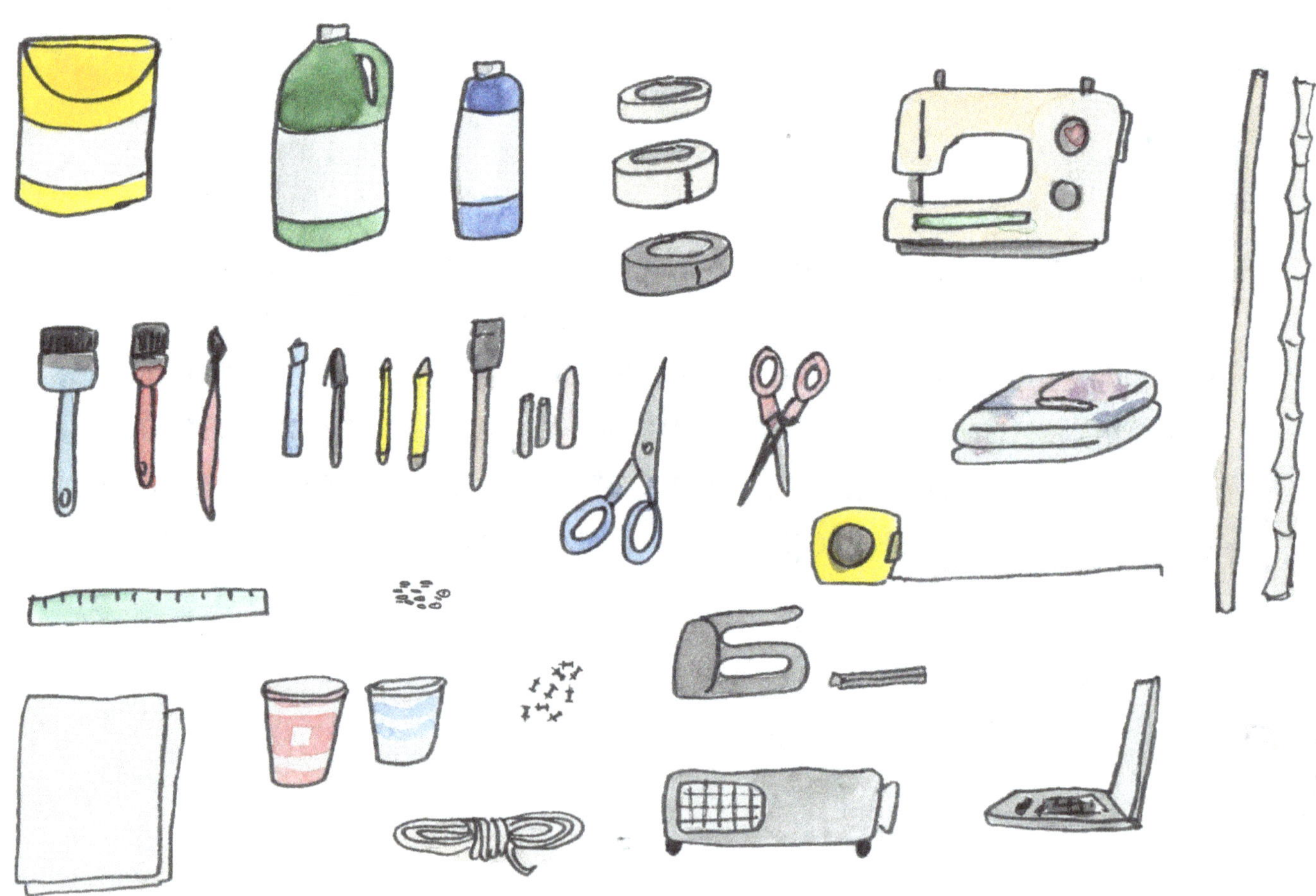

- **Latex or acrylic paint**
  Get bright strong colors of latex house paint or large (½-1 gallon) containers of acrylic. If paint is thick, thin it with about 1 part water to 3 parts paint, so it flows easily, but still covers solidly. You can pour paint into quart- sized yogurt style containers and use foam/bristle brushes of various sizes. Make sure to paint out any heavily painted areas where paint has pooled, so it will dry faster.

  Don't use oil-based paints because they are difficult to clean up, they smell badly and they dry slowly. Tempera paints aren't good either, because they aren't permanent and will run and wash away if the flag gets wet.

- **Paint brushes**
  Any paint brushes work. Use small brushes for details and big brushes to cover lots of space. You can use bristle brushes and foam brushes. Keep brushes in water or wash them as soon as you are done using them so the paint doesn't dry on the brush and ruin the brush. Use brushes that are in good condition (not frayed).

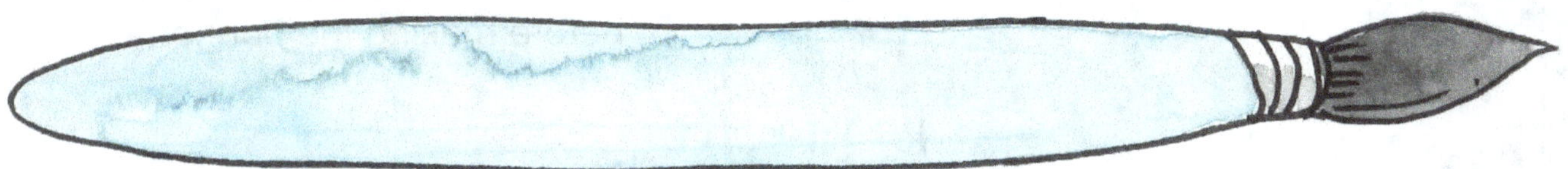

- **Paper** (for sketching ideas)
- **Pencil**
- **Chalk**
- **Permanent marker** (for outlining design)
- **Old yogurt or plastic containers and some lids**
- **Measuring tape**
- **Scissors**
- **Laptop and projector** (optional - if you want to project and trace your banner design)
- **Tape or tacks** (to hang banner if you are projecting an image or secure fabric on the ground)
- **Drop cloths** (to keep the floors clean and the banner from sticking)
- **Sewing machine** (optional - if you are making a huge banner that requires multiple fabric pieces being attached or want to sew seams for poles or tidy edges)
- **Grommets** (optional - if you want to attach to banner for hanging)
- **Rope** (optional - if you want to hang the banner)
- **Poles** (optional - if you want to mount the banner on poles)

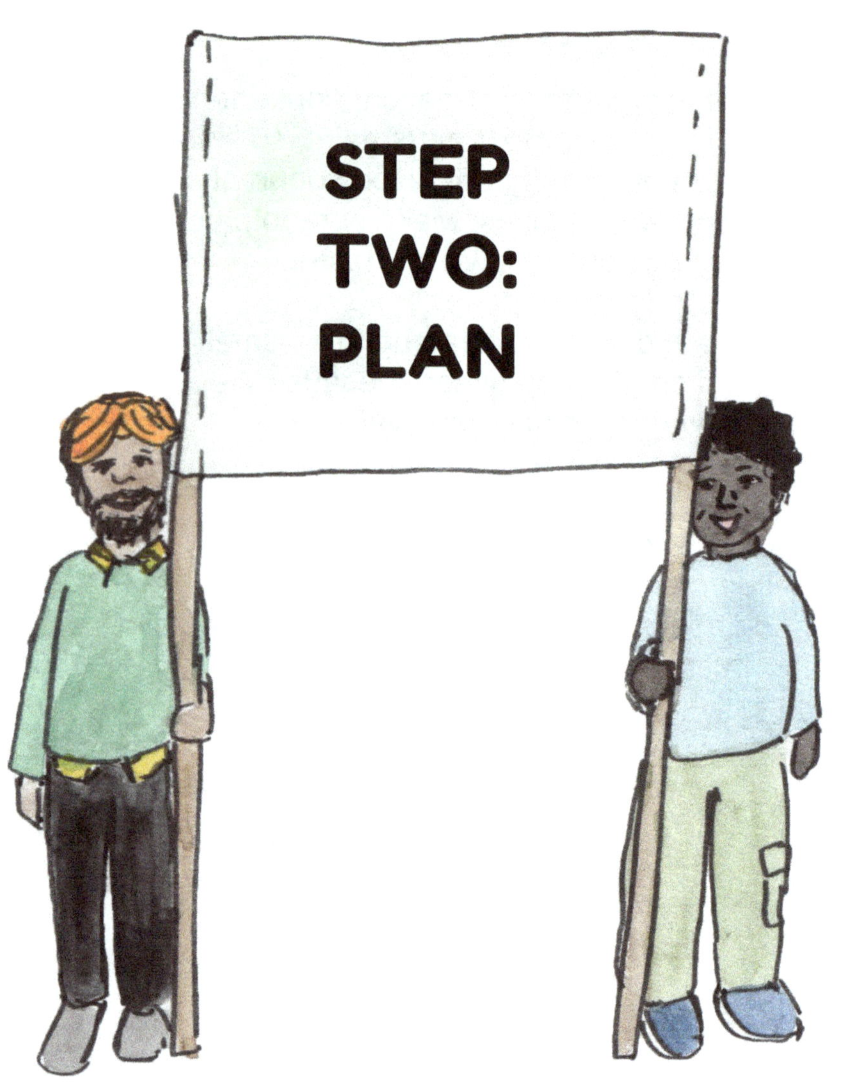

As you plan your banner consider the following:

Location: Where and how will the banner be used? What are the environmental conditions (high winds, wet weather, etc.)?

Size and scale: How large does the banner need to be to be visible, legible, and have an impact at the location where it will be used? A 10 meter /32 ft banner could look tiny if the scale of the background is large enough. Scout the location before making the banner!

Message: Keep it short and sweet. Test your message out on people before you commit. Make sure it makes sense to your target audience and to the general public, and not just insiders.

Time: Making banners takes longer than you think! Plan time for buying materials, construction, painting, drying paint, attaching hardware and rigging the anchoring or carrying system.

Budget: Is there enough money for the labor and materials involved? The budget may end up determining the size and location of the banner.

(Step Two: Plan text from Ruckus Society -
ruckus.org/training-manuals/manuals-checklists/creative-direct-action-visuals-manual/)

STEP THREE: SPACE

Try to find a large enough space to roll out the banner as you work on it. If you have a really huge banner, bigger than your space, paint one section at a time and wait for each section to dry before rolling it up and painting the next section.

STEP FOUR: TEXT AND DESIGN

If you are participating in a national or global coordinated event ,there might be slogans and graphics ready for you to use. Cut your banner fabric to match the scale of the template.

If you are creating your own design:

- Keep it simple with clear and communicative graphic elements and bold text.
- Use contrasting colors (light and dark) to make the banner easier to read.

- If you are painting a colored background, you can do that first, wait for it to dry then paint letters over the background. This is usually faster than painting your background around your letters. Have some backup work to do while you wait for the background to dry or take a break!

- Make sure your design or template dimensions match your banner dimensions!

Laying out your text by hand:

• Stretch your banner fabric out flat on the ground or on a table and secure the edges with tape, or by stapling it down to a large piece of plywood.

• Measure the length of the space where your text will go on your banner fabric.

• Give space on the sides for grommets, dowels, rope or other mounting or hanging apparatus.

- Count the number of letters (plus spaces between words) in your banner text.

- Divide up your total text space by the number of letters in your text.
  - Narrow letters like i and l can take half the amount of space and wide letters like w and m can take one and a half spaces

- You can mark out your 'spaces' lightly with pencil or with chalk

- If you have images or graphics account for the space that you want for those.

- You can size each line of text differently if they are different lengths, or if there is a main text and then a subtext.

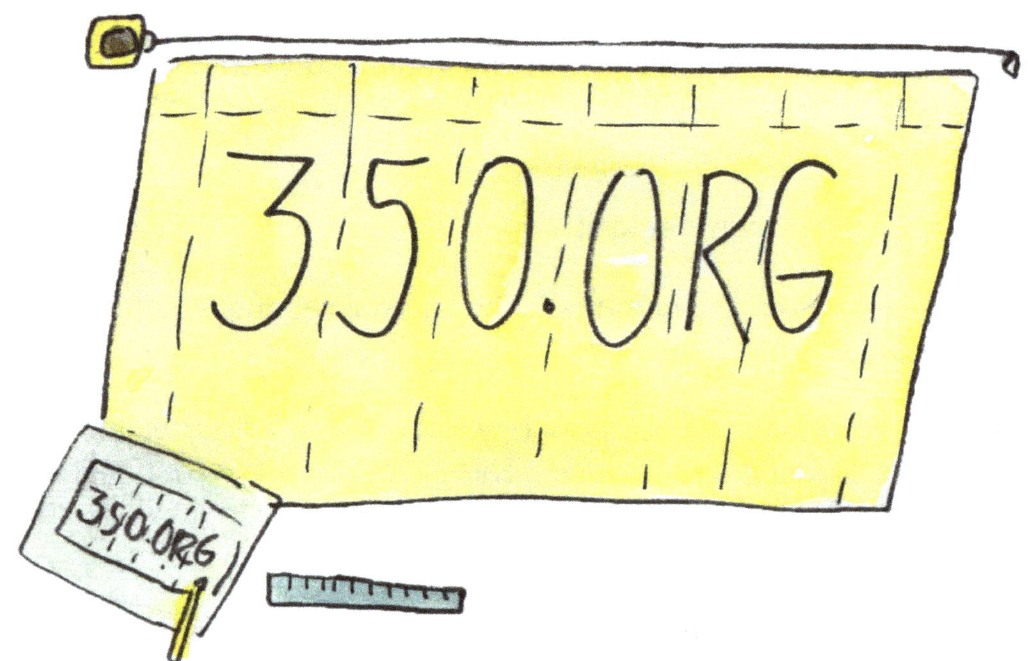

- Once you have your spaces marked, freehand your letters into their allotted spaces, first with pencil or chalk and then with permanent marker. (Chalk is nice because it can be easily rubbed away, but be careful that it doesn't rub away too soon! Pencil doesn't smudge, but can't easily be erased from fabric, so try keep the lines light.)

- You could also use a grid method to transfer your design. You draw a grid over your design on the paper, and then make a larger grid to scale on the fabric and then draw the design square by square onto the grid on the fabric.

- It helps to do your calculations and a sketch on paper first, scaling it to the dimensions of your banner.

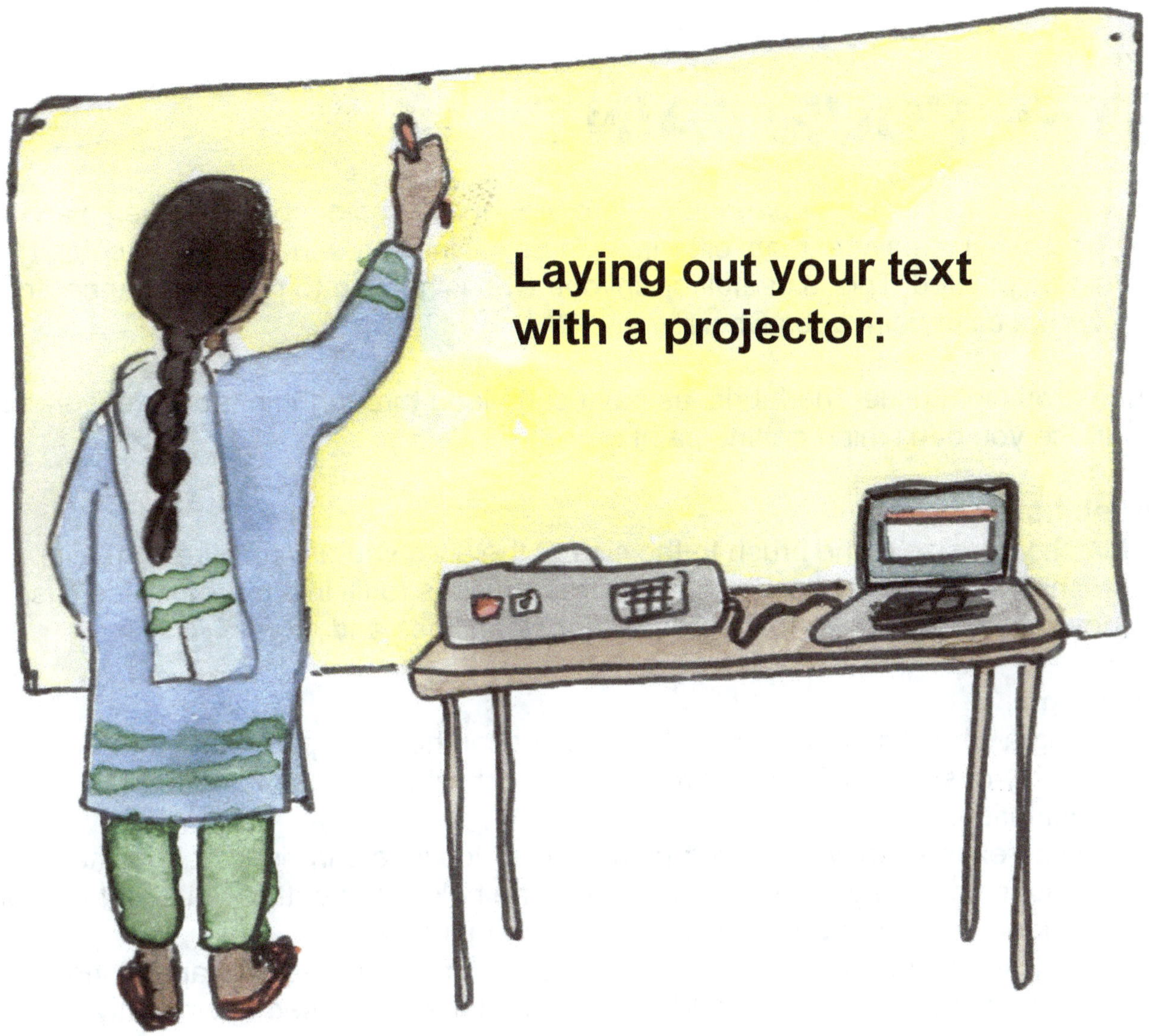

- Type and design your text in a word processing or graphic program on a computer that you can connect to the digital projector. Make sure the dimensions of your text design match your banner.

- Hang your banner fabric on the wall and project your text on the banner adjusting to fit. You may need to adjust the projector. If you are limited in how far back you can put the projector you can change the scale in your graphics program to get the image to the right size on the wall.

- You might need to trace your text in two sections. If so after you trace the first part, move the image over on the computer, then either move the fabric or move the projector, line it up again, and trace the last part.

- Trace your letters onto the fabric first with pencil and then with permanent marker or directly with permanent marker if you are experienced and confident!

STEP FOUR: PAINT

Now it's time to paint your banner. If there are multiple colors or a complex plan it can be helpful to have a 'map' or write with pencil inside each letter what color it should be painted. This is useful for anyone who is helping to paint the banner to know what color paint goes where!

Put a drop cloth under the fabric, as paint can bleed through thin fabric, or work on a surface you don't mind getting paint on.

Brush tips
- Match your size of the brush to the size of the area you are painting - smaller brushes for details or thin lines and larger brushes to fill in big areas. Use crisp (not frayed) brushes or foam brushes for clean lines and edges.

Paint tips
- Adding a small amount of water to the paint can help the paint run more smoothly over fabric. Test out what works best with your paint and fabric combination.
- You can experiment with mixing paint colors, you'll be surprised at how many variations you can get from a few colors. The bolder the better! You want to grab the attention and show how vibrant the movement is!
- If you want your banner to look extra neat, you can put masking tape along the lines of what you are painting. Make sure the tape is pressed down firmly to prevent leaks. Then remove the tape after you finish painting.
- Let the paint dry fully before rolling or folding up the banner.

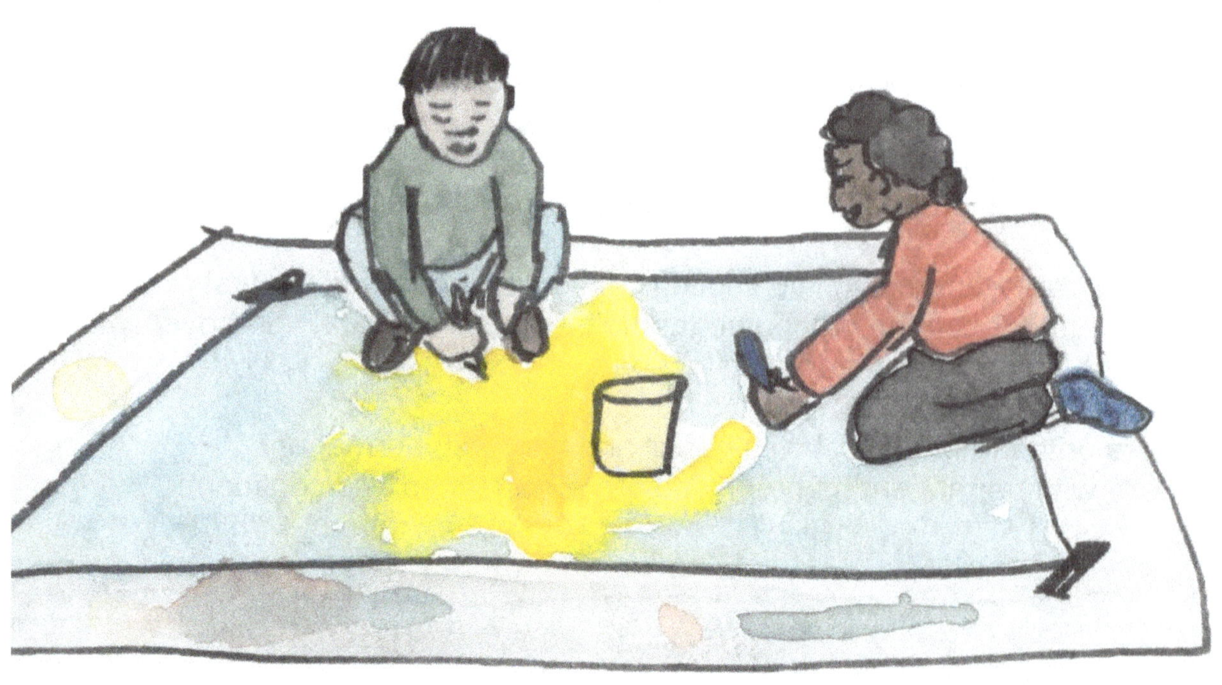

STEP FIVE: MOUNT AND USE

- Mount your banner as planned and get your message out there!

- If you will be carrying the banner in the wind you can cut small u-shaped holes into the banner to allow for the wind to pass through rather than struggle with a billowing banner in the wind.

- If you make several smaller banners that are visually similar you can carry them as flags all together.

- For more details on ways to hang banners (reinforcing, anchoring and hanging) look at https://ruckus.org/training-manuals/creative-direct-action-visuals/

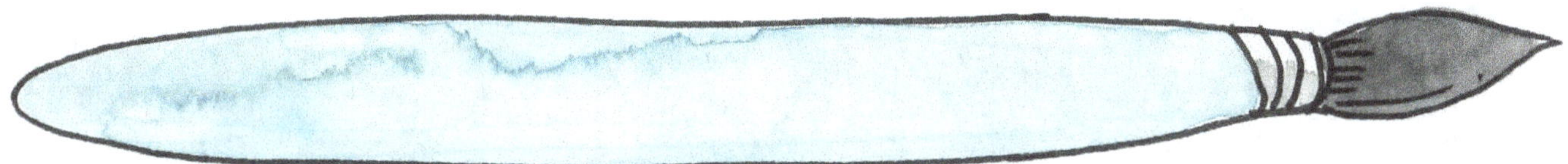

This how-to gives instructions for a painted banner. There are many other ways to make banners. You can make letters out of fabric, duct tape or spray paint. You can make letter by letter signs. While painted fabric banners are an important staple and very useful, there are also many other ways to get creative with signs and text!

9 781667 141374